THE STORY OF SOUTHEND PIER
— and its associations

*"Walk this pier with respect,
ladies and gentlemen, look
respectfully at the water and
the sands about for they have a
proud place in England's history."*
Alan Herbert, M.P.

The original coat of arms of the borough from 1892 to 1914, seems to have been unauthorised and called "a strange device", but at least it featured the pier!

FORTI NIHIL DIFFICILE

The present coat of arms, granted by Letters Patent, dated 1st and 2nd January, 1915, shows the lily and vase from the thirteenth century seal of the Cluniac Priory of St. Mary, indicating the parish church of that name at Prittlewell. The anchor is the symbol of St. Clement, patron saint of Leigh, while the gridiron is the emblem of St. Laurence, patron saint of Eastwood. The gold trefoil in the base is emblematical of the Holy Trinity, to whom the ancient church of Southchurch, once Seachurch, is dedicated.

PER MARE PER ECCLESIAM

With acknowledgements to the "Borough and County Arms of Essex" by W. Gurney Benham. (1916).

The story of
SOUTHEND PIER
...and its associations

E. W. SHEPHERD

EGON PUBLISHERS LTD
19 Baldock Road, Letchworth, Herts

First published in 1979
Copyright Egon Publishers Ltd.

ISBN 0 905858 11 5

Typesetting and design by
Art Anonymous, Langford, Beds.

Printed and bound in England by
Staples Printers Rochester Limited

To my wife Vera for all her help.

Chapter One

Picture before pier was built, showing houses erected in 1793, on what
is now Royal Terrace.

Because of the disastrous fire on the 29th July 1976, the fate of Southend-on-Sea's famous pier is once again in the balance, as it has been many times before, and controversy carries on in Council Chamber and on the streets whether to save or sell it. Piers are, by their very structure, vulnerable to both storm and fire, and there have been many casualties of both elements; yet unlike others of less durable construction dotted around the English coast, Southend Pier has been strong enough to withstand the fiercest of winter storms, although it was bad weather which nearly put paid to the first wooden pier built on the site one hundred and fifty years ago, when an exceptionally high tide carried away all the timber and other materials prepared for the project.

Shortage of money then, as now, threatened to bring the venture to an end before it had really started, "an undertaking which was the result of years of labour, thought and anxiety, which had provoked a prolonged and bitter controversy, keeping the people of Southend for a long period in a state of tension and turmoil!".[1] This was written all those years ago, but history has a funny habit of repeating itself.

The foundation-stone of the pier was laid in July 1829 in great style by the Lord Mayor of London wearing his ceremonial robes of office, as it seems the primary object of his visit had been to officiate at the seven year ceremonial at the Crowstone, [2], situated a mile or so away on the foreshore. Whether it was the most important function of his visit or not, the firing of cannon and the enthusiasm of the crowds added emphasis to what the majority of local people thought would bring prosperity to the place. For Southend was reckoned a quiet place for quiet people, where later, according to Punch, "only the wind took liberties". Now Margate and Herne Bay, which had already had piers, would face competition for the river traffic which was already of great benefit, especially to Margate.

Nothing stirred the imagination of the people in those early days, once the opposition had been overcome, more than the passing of the first pier bill through Parliament, due mainly to the exertions of another Lord Mayor of London, Alderman (later Sir) William Heygate, who lived locally in Royal Terrace, where Queen Caroline and her equally ill-fated daughter had stayed [3].

It was this distinguished lawyer who, when the mayoralty ended, in spite of his many and varied occupations, was consumed with the one great idea of a landing stage, for it was common knowledge that there was no place along nearly one hundred and fifty miles of Essex coastline from Tilbury to Harwich where boats could come in when the

William Goodday Strutt, (1762-1848) third son of John Strutt M.P. entered the army at 16 and served in the American War of Independence. Fought at the seige of Gibralter in 1782, in Flanders and the West Indies and was wounded three times, losing his left leg after service in Ireland, was appointed Deputy Governor of Stirling Castle and received by George III.

An unusual picture of the planned pier which appears not to have been accepted at this stage.

tide went out. But first of all, prominent land owners had to be convinced — not that they thought a proper landing stage was not necessary, but they did not want any inconvenience to themselves or their property — and there was, of course, justice in such an argument.

One of the first opponents was the lord of the manor, Mr J.B. Scratton, [4] who was concerned that any building on the Southend foreshore would damage his oyster beds. Gradually his objections were removed, but he still gave verbal assistance to the opposition while the oyster industry declined and by the end of the century was almost non-existent.

Another objection to the building of anything which would affect his view of the river was a formidable retired soldier, Major General William Goodday Strutt, who moved on to Marine Parade in Old Southend in 1824, and was afterwards connected with every move of the pier building. His daily diary of events, with one or two intervals, for nine years, was to prove invaluable in the pier's early history because of the fire which destroyed the House of Commons in 1834. The General's work cannot be measured in time but in the courage of his achievement, for he came to Southend at the age of sixty-two, having served with distinction in the Army overseas, as a result of which he was minus a leg and most of his teeth plus a bullet in his body which could not be extracted. He was seldom without pain, and was also troubled with gout. The late Lord Rayleigh, the head of the General's family, presented these records to the local Historical and Antiquarian Society in 1946, and they are now housed in the Essex Record Office at Southend Library. When the General obtained a promise that the pier would be sited at its present position, causing him no obstruction to

Major General William Goodday Strutt at 'Tofts', Little Baddow, where he died in 1848. To ease the pain in his severed limb his servant would make a poultice of the tobacco he bought.

his view from Rayleigh House, he removed his objections and joined the newly-formed company, buying shares in it with other members of his distinguished family, whose main seat is Terling Place, near Chelmsford.(5)

By far the most formidable objectors were the barge-owning Vandervords, who were opposed to everything which did not agree with their business activities, and this meant they wanted the site to be next to their jetty, opposite what is now Southchurch Avenue. Albert Vandervord had built the Great House, now the Minerva Public House, in 1793, and must have been of some influence, as the local manorial courts dealing mainly with Admiralty matters were held there. However, in spite of the following he had, the Vandervords did not get the jetty they had always wanted and which General Strutt had often advocated, for another twenty nine years.

Most, if not all these objections were aired at the Royal Hotel on March 3rd 1829, at a meeting chaired by Alderman Heygate (6) . So stormy was the debate that the chairman threatened to abandon the whole idea because of the expense and trouble it had already caused him. The Leigh fishermen, at first against the plan, changed their minds and supported the Alderman, and as a result two months later the Bill received the Royal Assent.

The welcome news brought out the flags and bunting, and when he landed on the beach below his house the one-time Lord Mayor was greeted with music and enthusiastic crowds, while some of the more energetic replaced the horses of the Heygate coach and pulled it, with the family aboard, through the Southend streets. Not far away from this particular celebration was a young painter, perhaps far enough away for it not to spoil his concentration. This was John Constable, living at this time with his nose in the creek at Leigh and engaged on one of his masterpieces — the painting of Hadleigh Castle [7].

Footnotes

1. General Strutt's papers.
2. The Crowstone marked the eastern limits of the jurisdiction of the City of London over the Thames from 1197 to 1857, when Richard I in need of money for the Crusades, sold the rights of the Crown for 1,500 marks. There are thirteen visits recorded by Lord Mayors of London, and their names are engraved on the stone, which was given in 1950 by the Port of London Authority to Southend Corporation. It now stands in the beautiful grounds of Priory Park. Another Crowstone erected in 1836 is situated on the fore-shore nearly opposite Chalkwell Avenue. Up to 1857, when the control of the river was vested in the Thames Conservancy Board, the mayoral visits every seven years were the occasion of festivities on the beach, and fireworks on the cliffs. The historian Philip Benton talks of "gorgeous water pageants".
3. Princess Charlotte, daughter of the Prince Regent, later George IV, and his wife, Caroline of Brunswick, visited Southend first in 1801. Three years later her mother, Queen Caroline, came for about six weeks, staying on what was at first The Terrace, then re-named Royal Terrace in her honour. The Grand also became the Royal Hotel. Both royal ladies had unfortunate lives; the daughter died in childbirth, and at least was spared the sight of her mother turned away from Westminster Abbey at the coronation of her husband. Rejected and discredited, this "queen of indiscretions" died soon afterwards.
4. J.B. Scratton belonged to a family who owned a great deal of land locally. Most prominent was Daniel Scratton who owned the Priory in 1927.
5. Major General William Goodday Strutt was the third son of John Strutt, large landowner and M.P. for Maldon. He built the present Terling Place. General Strutt's elder surviving brother was Colonel J.H. Strutt, also M.P. for Maldon, who like his father sat in the House of Commons continuously for over fifty years. His wife, Lady Charlotte Strutt, daughter of the Duke of Leinster, was elevated to the peerage as Baroness Rayleigh in 1821.
6. Alderman William Heygate was Lord Mayor of London in 1822, and was created a baronet by William IV in 1831. He was for some time M.P. for Sudbury in Suffolk.
7. John Constable's painting of Hadleigh Castle was originally called "Morning after a stormy night". Done in the evening of his days, it was exhibited at the Royal Academy but remained unsold. In 1838 it was bought by the artist's daughter for one hundred guineas. In 1851 it was purchased by the National Gallery for £320. Many artists have been attracted by this historic castle standing on a hill overlooking Leigh. There are said to be at least forty-two different prints of this painting.

Chapter Two

After the foundation-stone had been laid, no time was lost in getting on with the urgent business of building the pier. Not only because tolls could not be charged until 1,500 feet in length had been erected, but more urgent was the fact that powers under the original Act included the provision that the works would cease if not completed within five years. The outline of the plan contained five proposals:-

1. Construction of a pier and jetty or causeway from shore to deep water, where a flag would fly and a light be kept continually burning so that passengers and goods could be landed or shipped at all times of the tide, to avoid delay and risk of injury.

2. A healthy promenade would by these means be available to the public.

3. It was intended to construct, repair and secure certain roads, especially the main one which connects Upper and Lower Southend (more popularly New and Old Southend) which had been in a bad state of decay. Also to repair and build where necessary a road along the shore by the seaside to form a beautiful drive.

4. To open up a route to the parish church of Prittlewell, and

5. Details of dues and tolls.

All this gave a sense of purpose to the small resort, but few could have realised the magnitude of the task which had been outlined. Southend then was mainly countryside; wild tulip, mustard and mangel-wurzel, furze, broom and fennel grew along the cliffside, and cornfields and orchards reached to the sea. There were scattered cottages along the seafront mainly occupied by fishermen or farmers [1] and referred to by Benton as "Arthurs Land" bounded by the Thames farm on the east, "Porters" on the north and west, and on the south the beach or common. There had been a previous effort to popularise this part of the district, now Marine Parade. Some sixty years before the pier venture it was hoped to make it a convenient place for bathing, the situation being regarded as the most agreeable, but the project failed through lack of support.[2]

This was at the bottom of what is now Pier Hill, while above it a terrace was built with "commanding views of the estuary" in 1793, and here, where the wealthy congregated, was the New South End looking down in more ways than one upon the residents of Old South End. After the royal visits, the aristocratic tenants of Royal Terrace, having increased in number, worried about the resultant smell of decaying sea-weed around the timbers of the wooden structure, and how it would affect their delicate nostrils. One resident here, Lady Charlotte Denys,[3] was instrumental in the pier being sited where it was, for she sold the land necessary for the purpose.

In spite of the urgency, only three men were at first directly involved in building the pier; a carpenter, labourer and engineer. The committee had decided to proceed by direct labour. There were no plans as such! Other employees were taken on as the work progressed, but the engineer [4] was put on half pay, not out of any disrespect to him it was stressed, but of necessity. Once again it seemed that finance was the trouble, as Alderman Heygate had pointed out at the Royal Hotel. Before long the engineer's pay was restored, and by June the following year the first section of the wooden pier, some six hundred feet, was opened to the public.

The early struggles of those days are recorded in letters written by General Strutt to various members of the Committee of Management, who formed a formidable array of four baronets, two Members of Parliament, three directors of the East India Company, two members of Trinity House, and some magistrates who made up the shareholders, at £50 per share of the pier company. The prinicipal part in this syndicate was taken by the Heygate and Strutt families, for while the promoter and his family were wealthy local landowners, the General's family was influential around the Chelmsford area and in Parliament.

At a meeting in London on May 8th 1830, Alderman Heygate had reported to his committee that the first part of

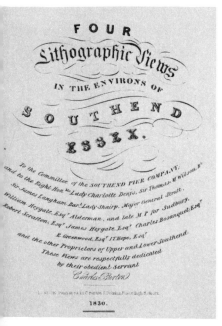

A tribute to some of the members of the original company who supported William Heygate in 1830.

FOUR
Lithographic Views
IN THE ENVIRONS OF
SOUTHEND
ESSEX.

To the Committee of the SOUTHEND PIER COMPANY,
and to the Right Honble Lady Charlotte Denys, Sir Thomas M Wilson B^t
Sir James Langham Bar^t Lady Shairp, Major General Strutt,
William Heygate, Esqr Alderman, and late M P for Sudbury,
Robert Scratton, Esqr James Heygate, Esqr Charles Bosanquet, Esqr
L Greenwood, Esqr H Hope, Esqr
and the other Proprietors of Upper and Lower Southend
These Views are respectfully dedicated
by their obedient servant
Charles Burton

1830.

12

the work was completed, and that a vessel named "The Clarence", in honour of the Duke of Clarence (in that year, William IV) was to be placed at the end of the pier or jetty, for the purpose of being used as a landing stage at low tide so that passengers from the steamboats could be taken from the Clarence by boat to the pier head or to the shore if there was enough water.

In the following year William Heygate was created a baronet by William IV, who sent his good wishes for the venture when the ship named after him was used at Southend. The honour was conferred on the Alderman after he had been Lord Mayor of London, 1822-3. He was also Alderman of Coleman Street ward in the City, Sheriff and City Chamberlain, a director of the South Sea Company, and Member of Parliament for Sudbury, Suffolk, for eight years. How he ever found time to promote the pier bill is a mystery, but his energy in its cause never flagged, and the baronetcy seemed encouragement for all his efforts. He celebrated too in the only way possible — on the pier, still in its infancy. Members of his family and of the committee attended, as did Major General Strutt with his brother, and the inevitable Lord Mayor of London.

Unfortunately, the good ship Clarence did not last very long in spite of its royal connections, but was towed back up the Thames. In its place, as the work progressed, came the lighthouse, or "Mount" as it was called, but the intrepid Leigh fishermen, who had in the first place been won over by the advocacy of Heygate, complained of it being a danger to navigation, and "Mount Misery" was their name for it, alleging that it was like someone smoking a pipe. As they then had a fleet of about one hundred and sixty boats, they were a force to be reckoned with, but somehow the Mount stayed where it was for a number of years.

Looking westwards toward the pier. The original of this picture was drawn on stone and was one of four presented to the pier committee in 1830.

One of the most popular of all early views of the pier 1831. Original drawn by Campion, engraved by H. Adlard.

In spite of all obstacles, progress in building the pier went on rapidly, so that by 1833 it had been extended to 1,500 feet. With this landmark reached came the most testing time of all, for the Act of 1829, and later that of 1835, stipulated that tolls could be charged when this length had been reached, not only on the highway, but also on water-borne goods loading or unloading three miles either side of the Ship Hotel. A toll gate was put up at the entrance to the pier and the harbour or breakwater alongside, which it was later alleged was hardly ever used.

Showing the pier and harbour. In the right background is St. Johns church while to the left is the library and Royal Hotel and terrace. c. 1840.

Now came the testing time for the whole concern. The pier company badly wanted the income to be obtained from tolls so that they could carry on with the improvements, not only out at sea, but on the highway which, in the original bill, they had promised to build.

Footnotes
1. The farmers joined in with the barge owners in opposition, especially to the siting of the pier, and the payment of tolls on their goods.
2. The History of Rochford Hundred by P. Benton. Prittlewell page 512, Vol.2.
3. Lady Charlotte Denys was the daughter of the second Earl of Pomfret, and lived on Royal Terrace. Her husband had already sold Leigh Marshes for £3,000 against £200 obtained for Pier Hill.
4. The engineer was Mr Walker, whose design and work on the pier was much admired. He became President of the Institute of Civil Engineers.

Chapter Three

The public were rightly incensed that they were forced to use the turnpike road leading to the pier, as the conditions in the Act had not been fulfilled. The only thing that was improved was the Royal, now Pier Hill, as it had only been a mere pathway along the Cliffs! Everyone grumbled, but only the Vandervords and farmers who had most to lose by the imposition of tolls, took more positive action, in which they were supported by Mr. Scratton, the lord of the manor, who contributed £50 to their cause. The barge owners agitated for a loading pier opposite where the Kursaal now stands, while the farmers wanted a jetty opposite the Ship Hotel so often mentioned by General Strutt, while the lord of the manor did not want one at all. So they had all lost.

Included in the powers to levy these dues on goods carried at sea to and from Southend was the authority given to the Customs Officer at Leigh to demand from every ship's captain a record showing that the required amount had been paid on loading or unloading goods. In attempting to dodge payments, and the Customs Officer, the barges landed goods at low water into carts. Before long there was, of course, violence.

Toll gates were broken up, and officials assaulted. The local magistracy seemed to side at first with the offenders, in the forefront of which were the Vandervords. Any attempt to enforce payment was met by threats, encouraged, it seemed, by the lack of support in the pier's interest by local Justices of the Peace. No wonder Sir William Heygate, celebrated lawyer that he was, exasperated by it all, was moved to say that the situation was without parallel in English legal history.

Yet General Strutt, still keeping his watching brief upon events, was able to write that "income has progressively increased by as much as could be expected considering the depression of the times". Yet the fact that he had called this period of 1833-4 one of depression was real enough. Agricultural workers were moving to the industrial areas in search of work, and this was the time when the Tolpuddle Martyrs were victimised as an example to the British working classes against militancy of any kind. The Government's policy did not succeed, for farm machinery was destroyed and haystacks burned down. Whether by accident or design, the House of Commons also shared the same fate, and the flames consumed the particulars of the Act of 1829, placing a much greater significance on the events recorded by the diligent General.

It is not surprising that the powers given to the committee, to erect tollhouses, tollgates and bars and chains on or across any part of the roads from Hadleigh to Southchurch met with such opposition, inspite of the fact that tolls had been applied to the building and maintenance of the highway since the time of Edward III. It was a sore point that roads were often in such a bad state of repair, yet tollgates flourished in the seventeenth and eighteenth centuries; there was said to be one every six to eight miles.

Even the essential coach service to London and to Cambridge via Chelmsford was affected. Each and every horse or beast drawing any coach was charged up to sixpence a time. This included every conceivable type of transport; landau, chariot, curricle, berlin, phaeton, calash, diligence, van, caravan, chaise, gig and even hearse. There were exceptions for mail and for any horse or carriage belonging to royalty, and this inclusion in the Act was not so silly as it sounded, for when the Hon. Emily Strutt lived from time to time at Rayleigh House after the General's death, she was visited there by Colonel (and Mrs) Maude who was equerry to Queen Victoria. He and his wife came in the Queen's coach, causing a commotion in Old Southend and envious glances from Royal Terrace.

There was also an affinity with Olde England in the list of exemptions of soldiers or passengers on horseback going to, or returning from any election, and knights serving in Parliament. Produce carried at sea covered about one hundred and fifty items, from wheat, oats, rye, barley etc., while the most expensive waterborne item was a corpse at a guinea! The living who landed by boat of any kind, which included watermen taking or putting passengers on shore, were subject to the rate of one shilling and sixpence each.

In 1835 the pier company was compelled to obtain a new Act for the furtherance of the work not completed, and naturally enough there were those who objected to any extension of time to finish the work. In the forefront were the Vandervords, who still complained that the promised jetty for their goods had not been built. [1] Complaint was also made about the harbour or breakwater being useless. There was, it was alleged, still difficulty in landing passengers at the pierhead at low water, and owing to the insufficient width, steamboats had problems making fast. The new Act was obtained on condition that the pier extension was carried into deep water, with the fixture there of a "good and sufficient light". [2]

The year 1835 marked the introduction of not only the new Act, but the recognition by the Admiralty that the pier really existed, for from this time on it was inserted on all charts of the Thames and its estuary. Perhaps the people of Southend should have been proud of this accomplishment. No doubt the majority were, but encouraged now by Dr Nolan, [3] the vicar of St. Mary's Church, who joined forces with the rest of the opposition, many demanded that the terms of the original Act had not been kept, because the roads were still unmade. They grumbled that tolls should not be paid. Strangely enough, it was at this juncture (15th October 1835) that the magistrates seemed to be having a change of heart, and at Rochford local watermen were fined one shilling each for not obeying the regulations. Yet it was almost another three years before a conviction was secured against the barge owners, who were fined heavily — for those days — at Wickford for non-payment of dues. Sir William Heygate was obviously delighted that the company's legal claims were at last being upheld, and that charges had to be paid for the use of the pier and its approaches.

By the middle of 1838, General Strutt made a further request to the committee that he wished to retire. Whatever his frustrations, he was getting on in years, being now seventy-six. Even then it took until October of that year to tell him that his resignation had been accepted. The pity was not that he was allowed to go, but that no word of thanks was uttered in the process. How he must have cherished the letter he received telling him of the meeting held at the Ship Hotel on Tuesday, November 19th, 1844, when it was proposed "that in the opinion of this meeting the inhabitants of Southend are greatly indebted to Major General Strutt for the interest he has taken in the improvement of the place by enclosing the Common and thereby providing for them and its visitors a good public promenade" (this remarkable and spacious promenade had been opened to the public at the same time as the harbour was ready to accommodate barges and other vessels). It was agreed that an address be prepared

The Ship Hotel from the beach.

The Ship Hotel was the centrepiece of life on what was then Lower Southend. It was the customers of this Hotel who wrote praising the General after his retirement in 1844

introducing the above resolution and that the signatures of the inhabitants be obtained on it, after which a deputation from the meeting would present it to Major General Strutt. It was also proposed and seconded that a copy of the address and foregoing resolution be forwarded to the editor of the Chelmsford Chronicle for insertion. [4]

The residents of Old or Lower Southend had every reason to be grateful to the gallant old soldier who, in spite of his handicaps, was able to sail his yacht "True Blue" upon his beloved Thames, where his sailing friends were the local watermen, whose attitude towards the payment of tolls distressed him. He had brought a certain amount of glamour into their lives, for he was the first person of such importance to live at the bottom of the hill. His home, Rayleigh House, which he had built in 1824 on what is now Marine Parade, had a frontage of 196 feet and was a substantial and roomy house with large gardens, stables and other outbuildings attached. Also included in the property were five houses and two shops adjacent. The pavement along this area was popularly known as "Strutt's Parade".

All that remains of the General's house is now a Restaurant called the Peveril in this picture. The pavement in front was called Strutt's Parade.

When General Strutt left Southend, because he could play no further part in the management of the pier, although he came back now and again, he must have felt as Henry Greville[5] did when writing about this place, echoing the old soldier's sentiments:-

> Sweet unpresuming little spot
> By some unknown, by some forgot
> Circling the friends my heart approves
> And rich in her it fondly loves
> Why must the dull affairs of life
> Drag me from thee to wordly strife?

Here at my ease from business free
My heart can grow as calm as thee
And like thy waves which gently roll
Unfettered by man's harsh control
Slide on unconscious as it goes
Unvexed by hope's incessant foes!
Then fare thee well Southend, farewell
thy woody bank
And long may'st thou remain unknown
to luxury or rank
Bloom bank for ever sweet to shade
contentment's friend
And long, ah long let reason seek and
folly shun Southend.

The General died at Little Baddow in 1848, living long enough to see the wooden pier reach out into the deeper waters of the estuary. His niece, the Hon. Emily Strutt, often took up residence in Southend until her death eight years later, when the property was sold for £5,320. His old house is now a restaurant, but the original owner is not forgotten. As chairman of the committee reporting at length on the progress being made in the construction of the pier, his clear and legible records — even to this day — must be his greatest achievement, and for this, his father John Strutt, MP of Terling Place, must take paternal credit. He would often advise his son then serving overseas to write correctly and with precision.

One of his letters seems prophetic in its vision: "Now let me once more press you to keep a journal and what appears at the moment a trifling matter may prove at a future day of consequence". And so it proved.

FOOTNOTES

1. A jetty could have been placed here, as there was authorisation in the 1829 Act for pier or jetty, not exceeding two of each.
2. The good and sufficient light was supervised then by Trinity House.
3 Dr Nolan was vicar of St. Mary's Church, falling out with his parishioners over the ringing of bells at 4 a.m. which disturbed his peace. Resultant court case led to imprisonment for members of his flock.
4. The Strutt Papers D/DS/128/9.
5. Henry Greville was a pseudonym of Alice Durand.

Chapter Four

St. John the Baptist Chapel, Southend. When this Church was consecrated in 1842 Southend became a separate parish. Major General Strutt gave the Communion Plate and table made from yew of Terling.

A committee was set up in 1910 and contained the names of many prominent people willing to help with the restoration fund: The Earl of Warwick, Lord Rayleigh, Rt. Hon. J. Round, Hon. C.H. Strutt, Sir T.F. Fowell Buxton, Major S. Carne Rasch, Hon. M. Lockwood, M.P., C.V.O. Princess Marie Louise was to open the fete but the death of King Edward VII prevented her attendance.

When the church of St. John the Baptist was consecrated in 1842, General Strutt again showed his generosity by presenting the communion plate and table made of yew from Terling to the new church. Southend was declared a separate parish from the ancient hamlet of Prittlewell, whence it derived its name being at the "south end" of it.

Prittlewell was one of the first settlements of the East Saxons, having emerged from a forest clearing in the sixth century. When the flag of the noble standard bearer of England flew over the ramparts of Rayleigh Castle (the only Essex castle noted in Domesday) the hamlet of Prittlewell was bound to be in the honour of Rayleigh with its pomp and pageantry on great occasions. Here the mighty

Sweyne — the greatest sheepmaster in Essex — held court, having built the castle after the Conquest, one of those erected to keep the invaders safe from the savage Saxons. Sweyne s son, Robert Fitz Sweyne, called Robert de Essex, chose Prittlewell as the place to endow a monastery, granting it and the church of Prittlewell to the Cluniac Priory of St. Pancras at Lewes in Sussex.

About this time Southend received much needed publicity from the "Spas of England" [1] which stated that "the Cockney who during the summer stops short at Gravesend in his excursion down the Thames, and is in ecstasies at that commonplace sort of retreat, can form no idea of the beauties he would enjoy were he to extend his steamer trip down the river as far as Southend, and stop on the North instead of the South Bank". The author had thought too that Southend folk would have reason to rejoice that Hockley Spa had been established so near to them, for most of the invalids who would have gone through a course of the saline water at Hockley in July would naturally have proceeded to Southend in August and September to take the benefit of sea bathing.

Even before its rise to a place of prominence as a holiday resort, Southend had been subject to the scorn of the journalist and the wit of the comedian. Only two years after the pier reached one and a third miles in length, 'Punch' complained that while the town was too small, the pier was too long. "Instances occur daily of a husband being at one end and a wife at the other end and never seeing each other for hours". That, of course, could have been more by design than accident, but the libellous inscription by the postman "No such place to be found" because he frequently passes the spot without being aware of it, seems to be overdoing the humour!

At this time coaches ran several times a day to London, and there were five steam boats daily in the summer, while barges belonging to the Vandervords sailed from Lower Pickle Herring Wharf and Stantons Lower Wharf on Fridays and Saturdays (according to William White "Essex 1848" page 101). It seems therefore that there was at least a certain amount of business activity in what 'Punch' called "a mere shrimp of a town".

Five years after this outburst, the unqualified opinion of a gentleman who visited the place was that the term "a quiet place for quiet people" could never have applied to Southend. The author of "Old Southend" dedicates his book to Alderman Brightwell, J.P. "in remembrance of many happy hours spent in his company during the editor's short sojourn in the Riviera of Essex" He then refers to Chambers Journal of November 1853, "quiet, dull Southend ...... with its half a dozen bathing machines and its two dozen or so bathers" and later he says "Southend is blessed with a beach as flat as a billiards table, which has necessitated a wooden jetty absolutely one and a third miles long. A dreary pilgrimage on slippery boards".[2]

Sir William Heygate, promoter of the pier, had passed away in 1844, but his family continued its association while General Strutt was nearing the end of his life at "Tofts", Little Baddow. The pier seemed like a ship without a rudder. But somehow the work went on, and by 1846 it was one and a quarter miles in length. At the end there were berthing places for three vessels, and at last the ultimate object had been reached; passengers were able to land and embark whatever the tricks of the tide. Also, it was the longest pleasure pier in England.

Yet, this was a year both of triumph and disaster, for the pier was in deeper water in more ways than one, for the finances of the company, which had been so ably managed by Sir William were now found to be non-existent. When the largest creditor demanded payment, the pier had to be sold. The first wooden structure, just seventeen years old, was bought for £17,000, changing hands several more times before it became Southend's own property, being purchased by the town's local board, as the result of the campaign launched by the enthusiasm of the "Southend Standard" [3] which was first published in August 1873. By this time, the railway had infused new life into the area.

For several years after the completion of the pier there was no great rush to the seaside, merely because the ordinary people had not the means of reaching it, for stage coaches were costly and out of the reach of the majority. So, before the railway line brought down the crowds, Southend was a resort favoured by the wealthy, who lived mainly on Royal Terrace, [4] and put their feet firmly down when there was any threat of intrusion to their normally placid lives.

They did this when the pier was mooted, and they did it again when a Bill was being piloted through Parliament for the construction of the London, Tilbury and Southend Railway, for with the final stage of the track running along the seafront to the pier, the Royal Terrace residents managed to have a clause inserted in the Bill to the effect that "no locomotive blows off steam within half a mile of the terrace". This put an end to any hope of the railway running along the Southend seafront on the last stage of its journey. As a result, the line after leaving Leigh and Chalkwell

Poster advertising sale of first pier, 1846, (from the original in Priory Museum).

stations, moved inland approaching Westcliff, [5] eventually arriving in the middle of Southend's busy shopping centre at the Central Station.

Four years after the Bill was passed, the first train steamed into the town on March 1st 1856. There had been many obstructions, such as the shortage of surveyors, for there were so many railway schemes that there were not enough trained staff to go round. When work started on any new stretch, property owners were usually hostile, and so were the villages "whose natives still live very much in the past, shrewd and suspicious". All newcomers were regarded as "furriners" and frowned upon.

A contemporary poster for the District Railway.

In the case of Southend it was the holidaymaker, particularly the Londoner who had lived so near the sea yet so far from it, for whom the journey there and back in a day had been up to then impossible. Now trains had transformed the lives of the people out of all reckoning, for within six years there were fifty-eight million passengers travelling on new tracks throughout England. Trade naturally prospered as goods were despatched quickly from place to place. However, it had not all been sweetness and light, since the early trains were not too comfortable to judge from "Punch" in the Third Class Travellers' Petition:

> Pity the sorrows of a third class man
> Whose trembling limbs with snow are whitened o'er
> Who for his fare has paid you all he can
> Cover him in and let him freeze no more.

In spite of the many complaints, and perhaps because of them, the railway authorities were well pleased with the popularity of the new line, which in the first place seemed not to be aimed at the seaside resort, but at Tilbury and the pleasure gardens at Rosherville, [6] which were then extremely well attended by Londoners. It could well have been the profits made by the London, Tilbury and Southend Railway that prompted the final lines from the same source:

> Oh from the weather when it snows and rains
> You might at least defend the poor
> It would not cost you much with all your gains
> Cover us in and luck attend your store.

The transformation of Southend from a sleepy resort holding little of interest to the building of the pier, and then the railway, was a gradual one, and eventually signalled the end of the tollgate and turnpike except on private roads. The type of visitor changed; by steamboat and coach they had travelled from all over southern England, but the railway brought them down from Poplar and Plaistow, Bow and Bethnal Green. They scorned the more peaceful pursuits of those "who had on yellow shoes, subscribed to the library, sailed around the Nore, fished off the pier and stared at passing ships". Fishing from the pier, it should be stated, has always been a popular pastime, and it provides a welcome income to its upkeep.

Three years after the railway came the School of Gunnery, opened at nearby Shoeburyness, then a separate parish, and here artillerymen acquired training and technique over the years, proving a valuable asset in many a battle. Such an important place required its own railway station, and during 1877 a Bill was prepared for this purpose, but was dropped when the War Department refused to approve it. Southend shopkeepers were grateful that Shoeburyness was not to be opened up, as it was feared as a rival to the holiday business. So the troops quartered there had to tramp along the seafront to and from the town, seeking refreshment at the appropriately named "Halfway House".

On February 1st 1884, in spite of local concern,

This poster appeared in 1895, and shows that although the railway line had been extended to Shoeburyness, the road had not been made up; so the public house suffered as a result.

Shoeburyness was relieved when a direct rail link was opened
with Southend. This was after lengthy squabbles on whether
the track should go over or under the roadway, but the
problem was solved by lowering the road and building a
bridge over the High Street, because it was thought that the
engines would frighten horses if trains ran underneath them.
Before long, the garrison town established a reputation of
its own with the quality of its guns and gunners, but more
to the local liking employment was found for many who
would otherwise have had to queue at soup kitchens or earn
a penny or two chopping firewood.

As local eyes were looking at the new invasion of
Londoners travelling to the seaside for the first time ever by
train, the historic link with the Crowstone ceremonial was
broken. This stone had marked the limit of the tidal Thames
and the control over it by the City of London since the time
of Richard I. Now, in 1857, the Thames Conservancy Board
took over from the city and managed it for fifty-two years,
when it was transferred to the Port of London in 1909, when
this authority became responsible for all aspects of life on the
river. Trinity House, on the other hand, maintained the old
lightship and all the coastal lights, including that of the pierhead, and to this day occasionally inspects the lights here

The Halfway House (c1903) on the
Southchurch/Thorpe Bay seafront,
it was aptly named, for it was much
used by gunners on their trek back
to barracks at Shoebury, before the
railway was extended there in
1884.

27

for effectiveness, and assists the local corporation in its maintenance. [7]

FOOTNOTES

1. The Spas of England, by Dr A B Granville M D F R S pages 614-617.
2. Essex in the Days of Old by John. T Page.
3. The Southend Standard originally published May 9th 1873, but the first copy extant is No. 15 dated August 15th 1873. This paper followed the Southend Advertiser & Literary Gazette published in 1868.
4. Residents of Royal Terrace included Baron Thompson, Lady Langham (who had planted a grove to the memory of George IV on the Cliffs) Emma Hamilton (Nelson s mistress) Sir Maryon Wilson and Lady Shairp.
5. Westcliff Station was opened in 1894 and Chalkwell after that.
6. The pleasure gardens of Rosherville were built in an old chalk quarry covering twenty acres west of Gravesend, and were the target for the tourist arriving by steamboat from London and Southend. There were varied amusements and dancing from 2 to 11 p.m. daily, and there was also a conservatory, maze, theatre, museum, baronial hall, fernery, and even a bear pit here.
7. Letter from Trinity House, 31st March, 1977.

Chapter Five

Locally the most important of all things on the Thames estuary beside the pier was the old Nore lightship, which was replaced during World War Two by the Maunsell towers when they were used as sites for anti-aircraft guns. It was a sad necessity for the Nore was the most popular of all seamarks around the coasts of the British Isles, its light being a symbol of homecoming for the returning traveller for over two hundred years, being described by Noble in his history of the Rochford Hundred as:

"Beacon of hope that soothes his sorrows past and marks the home that welcomes him at last."

Since 9th June 1943, this famous lightship has been in honourable retirement, being replaced by the Nore Forts.

It was first placed in position by a King s Lynn barber in 1732 and eventually taken over by Trinity House. As pleasure trips on the river increased it was something that everyone wanted to see: "Not a passenger steamer goes past that light without a tremor of excitement running through all that were on board. It seems as if there were magic in the name, whether for the sailor coming from the East Indies or from around the Horn, the cry is 'Here we are abreast the Nore' and the words have a sound that acts as a charm." [1]

Named after the Nore or North sandbank which is situated about five miles east of the pier, it indicated the seaward limit of the Port of London's authority. There has been a great deal written about it. One humorous poem called "The Boy at the Nore" by Thomas Hood was well publicised; two verses which run as follows:

"I lives with my toes to the flounders
And watches through long days and nights
Yet, cruelly eager men look
To catch the first glimpse of my lights. '
I never gets cold in the head
So my life on salt water is sweet,
I think I owes much of my health
To being well used to wet feet."

By far its most momentous days was when the naval mutiny centred around it. The mutiny broke out on the 20th May, 1797, and continued until 13th June, 1797, when all twenty one ships of the Nore Command dropped down to the mouth of the estuary and blockaded the mouth of the Thames. This revolt followed the Spithead mutiny which had been settled by this time, so that it did not receive much public support although most historians and many politicians found sympathy for the cause of the sailors.

"Old Neptune made haste to the Nore he did come
To waken his sons who had slept far too long." [2]

The factors which contributed to the mutiny were overcrowding in the ships, cruel treatment by some officers; short pay and poor medical facilities. All had its effect on men, who in many cases were pressed into the service; an example being Richard Parker who became the leader, being known by the grandiose title of "President of the floating republic".

The uprising gave the seamen a taste of freedom as they came ashore at Southend where they held convivial sessions at the Ship hotel on the seafront but it was a freedom they did not enjoy for long and some never again. For the leaders were sentenced to death, Parker being the first to be hanged

The Nore Forts replaced the famous old lightship, 9th June, 1943. After wonderful war-time service, the towers, of which there were seven, were eventually removed after a 'unique and interesting operation' by the Port of London Authority, the work taking several years.

from the yardarm pleading with his last breath, that his death might be the only penalty to be extracted by the government but another eighteen mutineers shared the same fate.

Several local men were involved in this affair, one of them Goldspring Thompson escaped by rowing boat in spite of being closely followed. He hid in ditches on Canvey Island for two days until the hunt for him was called off. The escapade did him little harm for he lived to the ripe old age of ninety-seven. He must have been regarded as something of a hero, for when he died shops were closed as a mark of respect.[3]

The mutiny failed mainly because the Admiralty removed all the lights and beacons from the river though the Nore light was kept burning as a result of a letter sent to the Admiralty by Trinity House, which read: "With respect to the Nore light vessel the Brethren are of the opinion that such a removal would not in the least prevent the mutinous ships from sailing, but as it is of signal service to any ships or vessels who may escape from there, they submit to their lordships whether it may not be right to let the vessel continue at her station and the light be exhibited as usual".[4]

The execution of Richard Parker

Trinity House has an affinity with Leigh for "the parish church of St. Clement of Leigh has many Trinity House connections". It stands on rising ground and has been a notable seamark for centuries. Now part of the borough the old fishing port was one of the first stations of Trinity House in the sixteenth century when it was a naval and trading base, in fact, it was the most important of all Thameside ports and a depot for pilots, who were formed here to work in conjunction with a similar guild at Deptford who took the vessels out while the Leigh pilots guided them in through the tricky waters of the estuary.

It was an act of Henry VIII which united the two associations when they became known as "the Fraternity of the most Glorious and Undivided Trinity of St. Clement" although some 400 years before this, Stephen Langton, archbishop of Canterbury, who had led the barons against King John, was the first to study the interests of those in peril on the sea; when there were no lights to guide them and robbers descended at will on those who were often shipwrecked. This far-sighted prelate founded a society of "Godly disposed men in the love of our Lord Christ, in the name of the master and fellows of Trinity Guild."

As there is no church at Deptford by the name of St. Clement, it has been assumed that the bond formed in the time of Henry took its name from the local church in which a tablet was placed in 1906 by Trinity House to commemorate distinguished local seamen who had served their country in war and peace, as masters and elder brethren.

In particular with the smell of the sea in their blood and in their names, the Haddock and Salmon families were the most outstanding, the former contributing no fewer than two admirals and seven sea captains — surely a record without equal in naval history. Born at Leigh in 1629, the most famous of the family was Richard — the Christian name favoured by the Haddocks — who became commander of the Royal James, flagship of the Earl of Sandwich. Richard was knighted and then almost on his own "doorstep" was appointed commander of the ships of war in the Thames and afterwards Controller of the Navy. During a period of his eventful career he served in the Victualling Office as a colleague of the celebrated diarist Samuel Pepys, who was master of Trinity House in 1676.

Admiral Nicholas Haddock. From a portrait in the Painted Hall, Greenwich Hospital, by permission of the Lords of the Admiralty.

At the battle of Solebay, Sir Richard had a miraculous escape, when the Dutch fleet more than held its own against the combined forces of England and France. The Earl of Sandwich seeing that the Royal James was sinking and being attacked by an enemy fireship begged Sir Richard, who had been wounded, and his men to get into the boat and save themselves, which they did. Soon afterwards the earl's flag-ship blew up, the Earl of Sandwich with it. In spite of this disaster, Sir Richard on his homecoming was received by Charles II who as a mark of his favour, took off the cap he was wearing and placed it on the captain's head. [5]

Captain William Haddock, son of Sir Richard, was master of Trinity House ten years before Pepys. During his office the Dutch entered the Thames and the king turned in his panic to Trinity House for advice on whether to sink ships in the river to hinder the enemy's approach. Before this expedient was necessary the Dutch were forced to retreat after attacking the Medway towns.

The youngest son of Sir Richard was Nicholas, who after brilliant seamanship and bravery at the siege of Gibraltar, returned to home waters, taking up the same post that his father once had as commander-in-chief, the Nore. Unfort-unately he had to retire prematurely from the service because of ill-health. To add to the confusion he had five sons, two of them named Richard.

A modern counterpart of these old sea-dogs and members of Trinity House is Captain Gerald P. McCraith, now living above Leigh cliffs with a splendid view of the river from which he has sailed all over the world. After thirty three years' service, he is an elder brother, chairman of light-houses and a Freeman of the City of London. In his office in the shadow of the Tower, he occupies the same room once used by Sir Richard Haddock, while keeping in touch with the illustrious servicemen and civilians of the present genera-tion. One of this company was the late Sir Winston Churchill, who of all the many pictures for which he posed, liked most of all the picture of himself in the uniform of elder brother. This great statesman could have paid no finer compliment to any one body.

FOOTNOTES

1. The Thames and its Story by Cassell & Co. ch XII p.356.
2. The Floating Republic by Manwaring & Dobree.
3. Goldspring Thompson was born at Canewdon in 1777. He had eight sons and daughters who left fifty grandchildren between them.
4. Trinity House by Commander Hilary P. Mead. ch IX p.72.
5. The history of the Rochford Hundred by P. Benton. vol. 1. p.352/5.

Training Ship Worcester from the Pierhead in 1869. It was used as the Thames Marine Officers' Training Ship and was anchored off the pier until 1871. Launched elelven years, previously as a converted sailing line battleship.

Chapter Six

The growing seaside resort was first recognised for its strategic value at the mouth of the Thames as it later was for its holiday traffic. This was on 25th May, 1863, when the naval authorities in conjunction with the army, organised an "invasion" of Southend. To defend it came the loyal army volunteer units with flags flying and bands playing from all over London and from Romford, Ilford, Brentwood, Hornchurch, Chipping Ongar and neighbours, Rochford.

Marching and counter-marching took place along the seafront to the applause of patriotic crowds who had been arriving by each successive train, assisted in this respect by steamboats and stage coaches who also brought their quota. The scene was set at Clifftown to the west of the pier where everybody assembled to see the "fight" between the blue-jackets and marines of the navy, under the commander-in-chief, the Nore, attempt to get the better of the defending volunteers, who were feeling confident in their ability aided by some big guns from the artillery garrison at Shoeburyness.

There was a great deal of activity and excitement when the bugles sounded the alarm as five naval gunboats were seen approaching the bottom of the cliffs early in the afternoon. In spite of a heavy bombardment from the defence forces the "enemy" made their way steadily up the slopes, capturing the heights with a final bayonet charge. It was all good clean fun and not a drop of blood had been spilt in the exercise.

Colonel McMurdo, chief of the defending forces, said he had been gratified with the whole affair, being so important that the volunteers should be acquainted with the best means of resisting an enemy. Three cheers were given for the gallant colonel and the commander-in-chief, the Nore, in which the spectators joined, bringing to an end a most enjoyable day for all concerned. [1] No one seemed worried at the ease with which the naval party had taken the cliffs, admittedly they were the professionals and it had only been an exercise but for at least three hundred years, this area had always been viewed with concern whenever war with the Dutch or French occurred because it was so vulnerable.

Three years after this event the local board had been formed, whose main concern was health, cliffs and pier. The members met at the Royal Hotel where everbody came in those days, probably because it was so conveniently situated at the corner of Royal Terrace and the High Street, over-looking the estuary and the coast of Kent. At the board's first meeting the combined post of surveyor and inspector of nuisances was established; before long this man was working very hard for his £20 per year.

At the Royal Hotel, which had been named previously the Grand and Capitol, social gatherings, tea parties, dinners and dances took place, including meetings of every kind. Even auctions were conducted here, as in 1868 when "Porters" was sold in ten lots, showing what a large estate it had been.

The first lot including the house, outbuildings, Lady's well and twenty-nine acres was sold to James Heygate, son of the pier's promoter who previously owned this property. Another ten-and-a-half acres were bought by the sister of James, so it seems as if there was an attempt to keep the historic old house in the family. This was only possible for a time and it is now the official residence of the mayors of the borough.[2]

At the time when Benjamin Disraeli came here in 1833, the tenant was Sir Francis Sykes although the owner was Sir William Heygate. At "Porters" the future earl of Beaconsfield lived with Lady Henrietta Sykes, while her husband was on a similar romantic mission abroad. Disraeli came to the town and found much to admire although he had travelled abroad a great deal. On his first visit he wrote that "I can answer to Southend being very pretty," while he called "Porters" "an old grange with gable ends and antique windows which Mr. Alderman Heygate turned into a comfortable residence and which is about half a mile from the town; a row of houses called a town."[3]

Ten years after his visit he helped to arouse the conscience of the nation with "Coningsby" and "Sybil" two novels which dealt with the deplorable conditions in which most people lived and the gulf that separated the two nations   rich and poor. Had he inspected the Prittlewell workhouse, only a short distance from where he was staying, he would have seen how the poor survived there, being unlucky enough to be either orphaned, widowed, unemployed or elderly.

This man who became prime minister in the most glorious days of the British Empire and a friend of the queen who called him "Dizzy" wrote as an author of the poverty of the people, yet his letter written on his second visit to Southend showed the elevated plane on which he lived while, at the same time, advertising the charms of the new resort: "I live solely on snipe and ride a great deal. You could not have a softer climate or sunnier skies than in much abused Southend. Here there are myrtles in the open air in profusion." [4]

Although residents of the district were pleased with the praise bestowed on it by this then aspiring author and politician, there were many who got their living from the water who would have liked some publicity into their plight, for in the latter half of the century the fisheries of the Thames began to decline. As they had been large enough to employ and rich enough to feed a tenth of the population living on its banks this was a tragedy. Strict rules governed the sale of fish and the size of the catch. An Act of Parliament stipulated that the master of every fishing vessel arriving at the Nore with his cargo had to report the time of his arrival and the details of fish that he carried under penalty of £20. Any marketable fish destroyed meant, if there was enough evidence, one month's hard labour. [5]

Because the railways conveyed fish cheaply where it was wanted it naturally became more popular than ever, resulting in over-fishing; this plus the heavy shipping and pollution of the river ruined the inshore fishing grounds, [6] forcing many Leigh men to go into shrimping, so that at one time there were nearly one hundred boats engaged in this industry, giving them a reputation second to none in this respect. There were others who did not consider this new industry worth the trouble in view of the competition from Holland and sold their boats. Some went to the Maplin Sands and Foulness and ran into trouble there.

As a result of casting their nets here a lengthy legal battle ensued over the rights of local fishermen to do this at what in recent years has been considered a possible site for an airport and/or a seaport but what was then, as now, used by the artillery as a firing range. Eventually the fishermen lost

A picture of Southend seafront c1865 with the pier in the background. This was about the time that Major General Strutt's house was auctioned.

the day and the man who adjudicated in favour of the Crown was the Solicitor General, Baron Farrer Herschell, [7] who had often sat on the steps of his father's chapel at Leigh while the elder Herschell had read the Bible to children grouped around him. The road named after the Rev. Ridley Haim Herschell is in west Leigh, south of the London Road.

Fishing was always a family business as it was decreed that no one could follow into it unless he had been brought up in the trade on the Thames or Medway, or served an apprenticeship in it. One man who had spent all his young life at sea on his father's boat until he became the pierhead master was William Bradley, who was said to combine the activities of fishing and smuggling, according to the opportunities available in both pursuits. In the middle of the last century Southend boatmen were said to "bear a bad reputation along the coast, having the character of attending far more to the acquisition of salvage than the preservation of life; and there are rival adventurers on the deep who do not scruple to call them wreckers." The writer admits that what was true in 1853 did not apply in the 1890s, when he wrote: "A finer and jollier set of fellows than the present Southend boatmen it would be impossible to produce; and it is a well-known fact that some of them have repeatedly risked their lives in attempting to save others." [8]

All this was true of William Bradley, who in deserting the sea as a fisherman lived upon the water at the end of the pier principally employed as a light-keeper, which meant that he had to keep a navigation light burning during the hours of darkness, having in the process to trim the wick of the lamp twice nightly. This was done by lowering the light into his house at the end of the pier, where he lived with his wife and three daughters. The roof was nearly always covered in seaweed but the intrepid William also used his home as his launching pad, often to dive overboard to save life, although the term "dive" is incorrect as he always jumped feet first into the sea. Whatever tactics he employed Mr. Bradley saved many lives, perhaps the most heroic act was the rescue of two boys, when he nearly lost his own, doing what to him came naturally.

In 1888 he was presented with £50 which was quite a large sum in those days, which displays the gratitude of the public who also gave him a clock, for his courage in many a storm. During one such episode a large barge smashed the old pier in two. He stayed at his station looking after the craft moored around his house, while his family were lowered to safety and taken ashore. His zest for adventure took him as coxswain on Southend's first lifeboat which saved twenty seven lives but willing as he was William had to give this work up as it interfered with his pierhead duties.

William Bradley (1850-1932) was something of a smuggler in his youth. Appointed Pierhead keeper at the age of 21, he joined the crew of Southend lifeboat. In both capacities he saved several lives. He joined Southend Borough Council and became an Alderman, serving on the pier committee.

This man of many parts was also on the town's regatta committee and local representative for the Shipwrecked Mariners Society. He not only saved human beings; by his many activities as a councillor and then alderman he served for many years on the pier committee, helping by his first-hand experiences to formulate the policy that kept the pier a financially successful operation. It's no wonder that his name is on the roll of honour at Southend's Civic Centre.

While serving on the pierhead he witnessed the arrival of Eugenie, Empress of the French, when she came by boat to visit her son, the Prince Imperial, then on a course at the artillery barracks, Shoeburyness. This occasion caused quite a flurry of excitement, everyone doing what they could to assist a difficult landing. It was reported that the empress, who was entertained at Osborne House by Queen Victoria, was in fine spirits not affected by the rough weather. Whisked away in tram cars from the pierhead the empress and her party were entertained at the Royal Hotel by the prince before returning to his barracks, where he had become popular because of his unassuming ways.

The *Southend Standard* carried this story on the 30th October 1874, having been first published in the previous year. Five years later it told of the tragedy that suddenly enveloped this family, with the death of the Prince Imperial in South Africa. He had ridden out on patrol with a force under the command of Lord Chelmsford, when he was ambushed by a party of Zulus. He had fought bravely and died heroically, the numerous wounds found later on him had all been in front of his body. Another Essex man, Brigadier, later Field Marshal, Evelyn Wood, V.C. who was to become Chelmsford's first ever freeman, had been told by the prince as if he had a premonition of his death: "I have no wish to be killed, but if it were to be I would rather be killed by an assegai than bullets, as that would show we were at close quarters." That was his fate and by a strange quirk of coincidence the horse he had been riding was called Fate.[9]

The *Standard* naturally published details of his will for he had been part of the local scene. In it he expressed his gratitude towards the Queen of England, the entire royal family and to the country in which for eight years he had received such cordial hospitality.

Acting as a sounding board for public opinion the *Standard* championed the cause of the pier. Such a medium was vital for a growing community and its longing for news as expressed by Cowper

The grand debate, the popular harangue
The tart reply, the logic and the wisdom and the wit
And the loud laugh   I long to know them all.

The paper received a great deal of support early in its life when it printed a notice from the local board which stated its intention, in the interests of the inhabitants of the district, to promote a local and personal Bill in Parliament for power to purchase the pier and to borrow the money for the necessary repairs to it. This was carried into effect and the pier was bought for the last time.

From a painting of the pierhead in 1890, where William Bradley lived for twenty years, in the process saving twenty seven lives.

FOOTNOTES

1. Southend-on-Sea District Historical Notes (1906) by John W. Burrows p 212/5.
2. "Porters" when sold was described as a very fine specimen of English architecture of the time of Henry VIII, with brewhouse, bakehouse, fowlhouse and woodhouse.
3. Essex in the days of Old (1897) by John T. Page, p232/3
4. Essex in the days of Old (1897) by John T. Page, p232/3
5. 33, Geo 11
6. The Southend Corporation had to pay heavy costs for polluting the river in 1907.
7. Justice of the Peace vol 9. Nov 7th. 1891.
8. Essex in the days of Old by John T. Page. p.232
9. From Midshipman to Field Marshal by Sir Evelyn Wood, V.C. Vol 2 ch 32, p.72

Chapter Seven

Now that the pier belonged to the local authority steps were taken to improve the facilities and the first item on the agenda was to improve the method of transporting baggage and stores over such a distance. So rail lines were introduced to help the poor old horse in its struggle to get to the other end. For a while a ride on this new railway was a novelty and proved an added attraction to the visitor, yet in the long run the horse was never entirely satisfactory and then the track was declared unsafe and the service suspended — this in 1873 as in 1978!

This position prompted a member of the local board to suggest that as the nag had proved such a nuisance, an elephant might be obtained. Probably with an eye to business he said that he knew the Prince of Wales had acquired one on his travels and was in the process of giving it away; what this wag did not make clear is what would have happened to the wooden pier when an Indian elephant had trampled over the boards a few times, assuming that the heir to the throne had been willing.

One of the earliest pictures of the horse-drawn truck. c1873

To replace the old horse, which had been sold at Rochford market, another was bought for £48 and shod with india rubber shoes. The service was resumed for there seemed no alternative to the ever faithful animal. Then another was added and they ran in tandem for some time.

Donkeys had been mentioned like the elephant and quickly rejected for there had been so much trouble with them and their charges, that the local board had held many a debate in an effort to curb their activities, but it seems that they were a national nuisance to judge from what "Punch at the seaside" had to say:

> The donkey boys of England, how lustily they scream,
> When they strive to keep together their donkeys in a team;
> And the riders who are anxious to be class'd among genteels
> Have a crowd of ragged donkey boys labouring at their heels.
>
> The donkey boys of England, how well they comprehend
> The animal to whom they act as master, guide and friend;
> The understanding that exists between them who'll dispute
> Or that the larger share of it falls sometime on the brute?

Certainly in earlier days General Strutt had his share of the boys' abuse when he and others of the pier committee were trying to implement the law regarding the payment of tolls and having to contend with a great deal of public agitation in the process. He wrote: "Even the donkey boys brave us, saying we have no Act of Parliament and they will do as they please." Which caused him to add a pencilled note to the section dealing with the prevention of nuisances, adding emphasis by underlining his insertion "donkey carts." He was not alone or loudest in the outcry against them.

Horse drawn car, 1886, they were a novelty but the track was declared unsafe thirteen years after this picture.

Old Pier — Southend 1881

Again the *Southend Standard* was the vehicle which carried many complaints of this nature persisting for many years. One letter in particular explains the annoyance and brings a reminder of these Dickensian days and could have been written by the great man himself; if he had not died four years before the date of the letter, which appeared in the Standard on the 13th March, 1874.

"Do you consider it conducive to a more robust or symmetrical growth," the writer asks, "that such choice plants as are now apparently establishing themselves without much assistance, should be exposed to the repressive action of a herd of half starved donkeys?" The local board did what they could in posting notices offering rewards for information received, leading to the conviction of the culprits while the donkey boys did what they could by tearing down the notices.

Like most troubles there were compensations; no one could deny the usefulness of the donkey when transport was required. The first such cart carried two or three passengers, one of the best known was owned by the Sharp family, who hired them out from a pitch opposite the Ship hotel. Later on rides for children were organised by Mrs. Sharp in Alexandra Road and circled what is now the bowling green. But this animal which has never been superseded as the children's favourite did have a rival for a while when goats were used, until being banned in December, 1894.[1]

The horse tramway on the pier although popular with

those who wanted to get to the other end, a novelty to the young, was not quite so well received by those who used the theatre when concerts first started on the pier in 1876. They were held in a covered marquee placed over the tramway, so that when a bell sounded the warning to artistes and audience the concert was suspended while the horse and its load trundled through. One account mentions this place in a not very flattering way "Southend pier not only enjoys the distinction of one of the longest piers extant, but affords accommodation to perhaps the smallest music hall stage ever seen, where during the season concerts take place within its canvas walls in the afternoon and evening." [2]

Again a number of ratepayers wanted to sell the pier and a deposit of £500 was received but the business came to nothing. It may well have been the wise counsel of the chairman of the local board who had prevailed. He was the Rev. Frederick Thackeray, known as "Joe" who according to his congregation was so good in the pulpit that it was a pity he ever had to leave it, even to attend a committee meeting! Mr. Thackeray was a cousin of the celebrated author, William Makepeace Thackeray, but his claim to fame rested on his own sporting abilities. His prowess was mentioned in *Tom Brown's School Days* by the Rev. Thomas Hughes. Mr Thackeray had played cricket for Cambridge University and the MCC, and was a good all-round athlete.

When he came to Shopland a year after his ordination as vicar of St. Mary's and curate of Great Wakering, he joined the local Milton cricket club, whose ground was between Park and Avenue Roads in Southend, now a built up area. In her *Recollections of Southend,* Miss Tawke wrote that the newcomer's social activities were not so well received as his sporting and other talents, for "he could always be depended upon for the latest information. He was a regular gossip column." Which may explain why he was so eloquent a preacher.

The Rev "Joe" lived on Royal Terrace where much of the town's early business must have been discussed. Anyone with a claim to distinction wore a top hat on the terrace and in this elite company most of them were members of "the top hatted brigade." One gentleman who had done very well in trade and determined not be outdone by his neighbours wore a gold band around his topper. Whenever he appeared the cry went up: "Here comes gold band!" [3]

Wearing top hats was normal practice in those days, even fishermen wore them going to church. Sometimes they used them as "balers" when out in their boats, but on Royal Terrace there seemed a great deal of snobbery in the habit, distinguishing the wearer from the common herd.

When he died Mr. Thackeray was buried in the now churchless churchyard of St Mary's, Shopland, in the same grave as his wife. Nearby his son who was drowned at sea also lies. This church was demolished in 1957. The wife of his cousin, William Makepeace Thackeray stayed for many years at Eden Lodge, Leigh, which was owned by Harvey Moore the painter. She was laid to rest at west Leigh.

Within the space of ten years, from 1880, Western Esplanade was constructed and new facilities appeared like the bank, a sure sign of prosperity. In the original court house the first petty sessions were held, while a much needed hospital was opened in Warrior Square, the foundation-stone being laid on the 13th August, by Lady Brooke, later the Countess of Warwick, who was a frequent visitor to Southend, her home being at Easton Lodge. Also involved in this project was a Dr. Deeping, grandfather of Warwick Deeping who was born locally and became a popular novelist. More will be heard of him later.

On the pier things were also moving; maritime signalling for Lloyds had started, while a new toll house was put up. In 1887, the same year that the hospital's foundation-stone was laid, work commenced on a new pier alongside the wooden structure. Twice within five years efforts had been made to get on with this project. Now at last it got under way, but not until after many hours of debate in the council chamber and arguments outside it.

The electric railway was opened in 1890. The first of its kind in the British Isles.

Another view of the original electric railway built by the Chelmsford firm of Crompton Parkinson.

Once the work started it progressed rapidly, so that the new iron structured pier although not completed was opened in 1889 to the public and finished two years later, at a cost of £80,000. This was not the end of the improvements for a single track electric railway was also installed by Crompton Parkinson, which carried goods and passengers much more effectively than the poor old horse. This railway established a record for it was said to be the first of its kind in Britain on the longest pleasure pier in the world.

On the new, much more substantial structure another theatre was placed, called the Pavilion. This was furnished with a piano and an organ and a boy was engaged at ten shillings a week to blow the organ, sell programmes and also to take money at the box office. When the organ was transferred to the local church of St. Albans, the boy was put on other work. Even the piermaster was not capable of managing the new pier, according to the local board of which he himself became a member. He was Mr. W.J. Chignell who was informed that he did not have the necessary experience. At least he had enough qualifications for the council chamber, for he became an alderman.

The piermaster's lot did not seem to be a particularly happy one, for he had to look after the foreshore as well, where there were a variety of problems, such as the control of boats and boatmen, the loading on the pier wharf, the Pier hill buildings, the sea defences, bathing huts and stations, the tramway and tolls on the steamboats, and so on. When he was given the task also of writing out day tickets for admission and told that he would be expected to look after the mortuary, the piermaster complained bitterly.

With the London, Tilbury, and Southend rail line firmly established and crowds flocking to the sea during the summer, many of the more affluent residents left, giving way to the noisy, bubbling enthusiasm of the working man, whose one idea was to escape from the grimness of the London slums, even for a day. To cope with this excursion rush from the capital another railway line was necessary; this was opened in October 1889, when the Great Eastern ran the new service from Liverpool Street. It was not only for holidaymakers, for many who travelled down came to look at the boom in housing that had developed to judge by the tempting advertisement: "From £5 per plot free-hold, the finest, highest, choicest, best and cheapest sites at Southend-on-Sea, Westcliff, Leigh-on-Sea Rayleigh, Prittlewell, Rochford, Pitsea, Laindon, Shoeburyness. Auction sales three times a week during the season." [4] The advertisement was placed by the Land Company, 67/68 Cheapside, London, E.C. and appeared in the local papers.

Before this new link had been opened there had been a great deal of criticism of the old, to judge from the following: "There is one drawback to Southend, and in truth a somewhat serious one. The service of trains is by no means all it should be, and the arrangements generally at the squalid Fenchurch Street station are simply deplorable. The fares are low but little else can be said in favour of the line." [5] To judge from the views expressed by present day commuters, nothing has changed, except the fares.

On 19th September, 1892, the town received its charter as a municipal borough, so ending local board government after twenty six years. This brought about the union of the old with the new — the ancient hamlet of Prittlewell with the bustling, sprawling Southend. Bands played as soldiers and lifeboatmen, fishermen and firemen, mayors of Essex and sheriffs of London, marched in procession through the decorated streets, cheered on by children excited by the event and the fact that they had been given a day away from school; with a medal to each, marking this rare show of civic

PIER PAVILION,
SOUTHEND-ON-SEA.

MR. W. G. BEGLEY,
BEGS TO ANNOUNCE A

GRAND EVENING CONCERT,
BY ARRANGEMENT WITH

Mr. PERCY NOTCUTT,
(OF THE MUSICAL EXCHANGE, LONDON.)

Monday, Sept. 30th, 1895, to Commence at 8 o'clock

DOORS OPEN AT 7.15.

Entry by Special door for all Seats booked prior to September 30th.

MR. SIMS REEVES.

Soprano, Miss EDITH BARRY.
Tenor, Mr. TREFELYN DAVID.
Baritone, Mr. ARTHUR BARRY.
Basso Profundo, Mr. ALEXANDER TUCKER.
Solo Violinist, Miss LOUISE NANNEY.
("LAUREATE" OF THE BRUSSELS CONSERVATOIRE.)
Solo Pianoforte, The CHEVALIER B. PALMIER.
(PIANIST TO THE COURT OF GREECE.)

**RESERVED SEATS 5s. SECOND SEATS 3s.
THIRD SEATS 2s.**

A LIMITED NUMBER OF SEATS AT 1s.

Tickets and Plan of the Hall at VAL. MASON'S Alexandra Street.

The Pavilion was built with the iron pier in 1889 and this was the programme on 30th September, 1895.

49

SOUTHEND-ON-SEA, ESSEX,

Immediately adjoining the New Hamlet Station on the London, Tilbury and Southend Railway, West-end of the Town, facing South, close to the Sea, 50 minutes from London. Two lines of Railway.

SALE of FORTY PLOTS of

RIPE FREEHOLD

BUILDING LAND,

— AND —

SEVEN Well-built and Tastefully Designed

RESIDENCES

(ALL LET), with direct access to the Shore, within five minutes of the new Hamlet Railway Station, contiguous to the Cliff Town part of the Borough of Southend-on-Sea, being

THE FIRST PORTION OF

The "Hamlet" Estate, Southend.

THIS property is charmingly situate on ground facing South and rising gradually from the Cliff, it is beautifully Timbered, and commands an extensive prospect of the estuary of the Rivers Thames and Medway, and the Coast of Kent, and the constant passing of Vessels of various tonnages and nationalities, to and from all parts of the world, gives life and animation to the scene and combines to form a panorama not to be easily equalled. The salubrity of the climate is well known, and the walks and drives in the vicinity are varied and beautiful. The Esplanade at the bottom of the Cliff furnishes a most agreeable Promenade along the water-side, either to the Pier or to Leigh. The estate is within two minutes' walk of the Hamlet Station, ten minutes of the Southend Station of the London, Tilbury and Southend Railway, and eighteen minutes from the Station of the Great Eastern Railway.

The London, Tilbury and Southend Railway Company have informed the Vendors that the greater number of the Trains now running to and from Southend shall be stopped at the New Hamlet Station, including the 9 o'clock Morning Express from Southend to London, and the 5.15 down Express.

Possession of the Building Plots will be given on payment of 10 per cent. deposit; the balance of Purchase-money to be paid on completion of Purchase, or, at the option of the Purchasers, by the deferred payments mentioned in the Conditions of Sale.

THESE PLOTS OFFER ADMIRABLE SITES FOR MEDIUM-CLASS VILLAS,

And will be Sold by Auction, by

Mr. W. V. WILLSON,

IN A MARQUEE ON THE ESTATE,

On SATURDAY, the 11th day of MAY, 1895,

AT HALF-PAST TWO O'CLOCK IN THE AFTERNOON.

Plans, Particulars [and Conditions of Sale may be obtained of Messrs. W. & F. GREGSON, Solicitors, Southend-on-Sea; of Messrs. TAPP & JONES, Land Agents and Surveyors, 15, Great George Street, London, S.W.; or of

The Auctioneer, Southend-on-Sea.

Westcliff railway station is referred to here as the "New Hamlet Station" and had been opened a year before this advertisement of 1895 appeared. There was an attempt to change the name of Westcliff for 'Kensington-on-Sea' and a board was put up to this effect.

pride and pageantry.

The mounted police led the way followed by the City Marshal, the Burnham brass band and the band of the Royal Artillery, Shoeburyness, then came the fire brigades of Leytonstone, Grays, Edmonton, Barking and Brentwood, followed by the Leicestershire Regiment, the Oddfellows, religious bodies and temperance societies. Bringing up the rear was the Lord Lieutenant and Chief Constable of Essex and the mayors of the county towns of West Ham, Saffron Walden, Colchester, Chelmsford, Maldon, Clacton, Grays, Halstead, Ilford, Leyton, Walthamstow and Woodford.

Southend-on-Sea received its charter as a municipal borough on 19th September 1892, and the Lord Mayor of London is here seen walking in procession on the pier, which then used the new borough's coat of arms, until 1914.

In all that gathering, though they were hardly noticed as they marched along, were the representatives of the Medway Steam Packet Company and the General Steam Navigation Company, the two companies that played a large part in the life of the pier helping it survive financially, by bringing their pleasure boats to Southend. The captains of these steamboats, by calling at other seaside resorts and tying up at their piers, were able to suggest improvements to berthing facilities at Southend which were to prove of great value.

One of these companies suggested that dredging at the pierhead would solve some of the difficulties in berthing arrangements and the pier committee of the newly-constituted municipal borough council, which met for the first time on 9th November, 1892, was sufficiently interested to ask for the costs of such a scheme, which would provide a greater depth of water at low tide. The piermaster said he had seen nothing on his travels which would answer for the "sucker" system then used at Liverpool. At a special meeting plans for enlarging the pierhead were discussed on the 20th November, 1895, but the proposals were not carried, mainly because of the objections of the Leigh fishermen who did not want a longer pier at any price. They tried to enlist the support of the Board of Trade against the extension of the pier, but they were unsuccessful. In any case Southend Corporation was then bound to try dredging in spite of the fact that the sand would silt up again and again, while the dredger itself would cost £20,000, which would have to be maintained all the year round with a crew of men adding to the expense. There seemed a strong feeling that the extension would only be justified when all other means had failed.

Captain Kelly, the piermaster, was adamant that the cheapest and most effectual remedy was to lengthen the pier. He was very likely thinking of the shambles that sometimes existed when the passengers came off the boats, getting confused with those attempting to get on, all struggling in the gangway with nothing between them and deep water but a chain. A local paper described the official reaction : "Captain Kelly tears his hair and the Pier Committee with the clerk rides along on the tram shouting, 'Something must be done' ".(6)

Two years later the extension was made after the report by Mr (later Sir) James Brunlees, the engineer who had so much to do with the maintenance of it all. He now became involved in the scheme to extend the pier northwards, including the provision of a bandstand and increased shelter and refreshment room accommodation.

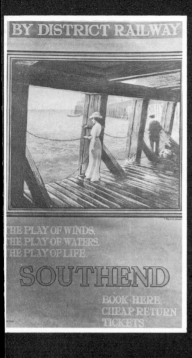 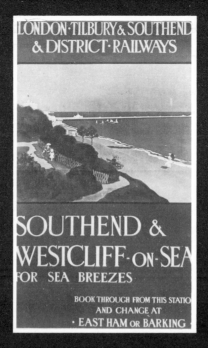 

Examples of railway posters used to encourage visitors to Southend and district.

FOOTNOTES

1. The Tramways of Southend by V.E. Burrows. ch 1. p.15.
2. Dicken's Dictionary of the Thames. p.196
3. Recollections of Southend-on-Sea by Miss Tawke. ch.1. p.8.
4. Remarks May 1895.
5. Dicken's Dictionary of the Thames. p.196.
6. Remarks. June 1895.
7. Mr (later Sir) James Brunlees built first portion while the pier extension was constructed by John Brunlees and Sir John Darry.

'Crested Eagle' — the first Thames pleasure steamer to be fitted for burning oil. It was used as a floating grandstand on the Thames for viewing the Coronation procession in 1937. She sank while taking part in the Dunkirk evacuation in June 1940.

Chapter Eight

'Royal Sovereign', another casualty of enemy action, being sunk by a mine in the Bristol Channel December 1940.

There was much to engage the attention of the committee and fortunately it was not always on the debit side. The London, Woolwich and Clacton Co., who had complained at the late start of the trams on Sunday mornings, wrote saying that the directors had decided to name their steamer then being built the "Southend Belle". Naturally enough the town clerk was asked to express the committee's satisfaction at the proposal.

Just as the pier is the centrepiece indelibly linked with the borough, so the steamer has always been considered as part of the holiday scene. It had been almost a magical transformation, for before the pier reached deep water passengers landing from boats had to wait for the vans sent out from the Royal and Ship Hotels. The journey was said to be "like going to Tyburn in a cart"[1], although the first experiment of a barge fitted with a steam engine took place just after the turn of the century, in 1801.

Thirty years after this trial there were over fifty pleasure craft plying for hire on the Thames as the pier was feeling its way out into the estuary. These boats, towards the middle of the last century, were owned by fifteen steamboat companies who worked their vessels on the Thames and in coastal waters. Of these the General Steam Navigation Company was the oldest in terms of sea-going boats. Their earliest were the Eagle and Eclipse, both built in 1820. Two years later came the Royal Sovereign followed by the Magnet. This company acquired other boats in between times but the Eagle and Royal Sovereign are names still nostalgically remembered by happy holidaymakers who were able to travel on them to Margate, Herne Bay, Clacton and beyond.

The 'Magnet' was one of the earliest steam packets to call at Southend, leaving St. Katherine's at 10 a.m., every weekday, she also visited Chatham and Sheerness c 1834.

The company, appreciating the popularity of these boats, repeated the names on others that followed. The second Eagle was bought in 1856 and she remained in service for some thirty years, being identified upon the river with her distinctive colours: funnel painted black, white paddle boxes and red wheels, with her lifeboats a deep blue. She certainly brought colour to a sometimes dreary river. However much their appearance attracted most people, the fishermen were not a bit enthralled with these boats, seeing in the churning waters that they made, a certain threat to their livelihood, which had suffered through the scarcity of fish caused by contamination. To make their feelings plain they would row their vessels across the path of these "intruders" and lay on their oars, often at the risk of their lives.

There was one boat the fishermen were particularly concerned about, this was the "Kingfisher", the fastest excursion boat built up to this time (1906). Her speed, just over 21 knots, caused many claims to be brought against the company from the owners of small craft who couldn't get out of the way in time and were swamped by the big ship's wash. No doubt because of the complaints the "Kingfisher" did not last long on the river and was sold for work in the Adriatic, finishing her career in Hong Kong.

"Kingfisher" arriving at the pier-head 10th September, 1908. This boat lacked manoeuvrability when going alongside piers and the terrific wash she created when travelling fast, outweighed the advantage of her high speed of 21 knots.

Gradually the fishermen accepted the inevitablility of the whole business as holidaymakers poured into Southend, many who obviously made for the pier and sampling the salt sea spray in their faces came again and again, for it was a world away from all they had known before. As John Masefield wrote:-

> I must go down to the seas again for the call of the running tide
> Is a wild call and a clear call that cannot be denied;
> And all I ask is a windy day with the white clouds flying
> And the flung spray and the blown spume and the seagulls crying.

So popular had the steamboat become that the Board of Trade complained about the overcrowding on them, to which the town clerk replied that only the number of passengers went on board as were allowed by the respective captains. This of course passed the buck into the court of the steamship companies, who could not have been unmindful of the dreadful disaster in the river on the 3rd September 1878, when the Princess Alice was struck by the Bywell Castle with the loss of seven hundred lives; the worst river tragedy ever recorded in the British Isles.

The 'Kingfisher' leaving the pier on the same day, showing her terrific wash, which upset — in more ways than one - the local fishermen.

A common sight before, between and after the two world wars — the decks of both the pier and steamboats awash with people.

The M.V. "Crested Eagle" was built at Sunderland in 1932.

Yet it was natural enough to carry the maximum passengers allowed, for many companies were finding it difficult to survive. One of these was Palace Steamers, who in spite of having two of the best known pleasure boats were unable to pay the instalments due to the builders. These were the Koh-i-noor and La Marguerite, built between 1892 and 1894. Entirely of steel, the Koh-i-noor was considered almost unsinkable being divided into watertight compartments. She travelled from Old Swan pier to Southend and Clacton. It was most luxurious for those days, with electric light, a post office, hair dressing establishment, bathrooms, book and fruit stalls.

Maintaining this high standard may well have been the cause of the company's eventual downfall, for that great favourite La Marguerite was even more superbly fitted out. It was also faster than the Kingfisher — so more of a nuisance to fishermen — making the trip to Boulogne from Tilbury and return in the same day. For ten seasons it continued to the delight of all, and then La Marguerite was transferred to the coast of North Wales where she was just as much in demand. With the outbreak of World War One she was taken over by the Admiralty and used as a troop transporter between Southampton and the French ports, carrying over 360,000 servicemen in the process.

Another of the important concerns was the Medway Steam Packet Co., later the New Medway Steam Packet Co., who asked for a reduction in the tolls paid by them in respect of passengers landing and embarking. This request was refused but it was a sign of the times. Competition was getting fierce as society becoming more affluent demanded higher standards, so the smaller companies fell by the wayside and the larger firms inherited their business, although some of these succumbed. Clacton pier refused to allow one company to carry on using their facilities as outstanding dues had not been paid, while at Southend a local agent for a firm feeling the pinch asked for a free pass on the pier. He was kept in suspense when the committee decided to reconsider the matter and finally turned his request down.

Another boat remembered with affection — the Medway Queen, 1924 was first used between Rochester and Southend.

In 1900 a royal commission inquired into the state of the river which since 1857 had been the responsibility of the Thames Conservancy Board, who had not been able to improve the channels to what was required, apparently because they did not have the means to do so. There had been a great deal of contamination which certainly did not go unnoticed by the pungent "Punch":-

Filthy river, filthy river
Foul from London to the Nore,
What are thou but one vast gutter
One tremendous common shore.

At work on the pier extension,
22nd May, 1905...

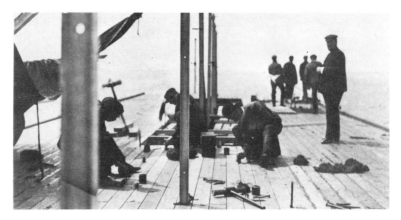

...and on 9th July, 1908.

Workmen busy on the pier extension on 9th July, 1908, the upper
deck of which was opened to the
public sixteen days after this date.

1908 — Holidaymakers sampling the new extension just completed, while the flag of The General Steam Navigation Company, the oldest sea-going company in the world, flies overhead.

Two years after this inquiry it was decided that the Thames should be placed into the hands of a port authority, but it was not until 31st March 1909, that the Port of London Authority took over responsibility for the seventy miles of tidal water from Teddington to the Nore. Before that happened Southend in 1907 had to pay costs and damages amounting to £9,500 for discharging its sewage into the estuary, although its method of disposal had been previously sanctioned by the Board of Trade.

The Port of London Authority had taken on a tremendous task, including not only pollution but navigation and regulation of river traffic; surveying and charting and the removal of all kinds of wrecks. Perhaps most important of all was the maintenance of adequate river channels. This gigantic task was carried out when fifty million tons were dredged from the river bed producing the world's largest deep sea channel.

Essex has much to be grateful for in this achievement, for there is thirty miles of the county's coastline from Bow creek to the Crowstone affected by this improvement, although the jurisdiction of the P.L.A. now extends to Havengore. This river is now cleaner than it has been for centuries in spite of the cargo ships and oil tankers that ply on its waters with the regularity of vehicles on the motorway. Yet, there had been no spectacle to equal that which was about to descend upon the estuary.

FOOTNOTE

1.   Southend Pier and its story, by John W Burrows, F.S.A. p.19.

Chapter
Nine

When the Home and Atlantic fleets entered the river on 17th July 1909, nothing like this formidable force of ships had ever been seen in the Thames before. One hundred and fifty vessels altogether, of which only the smaller craft were able to find enough water to steam on to Gravesend and Westminster, leaving the battleships, cruisers, destroyers and submarines anchored in parallel lines from Southend beyond the Nore. These were commanded by Admiral Sir W.H. May, in charge of the Home Fleet, while the commander of the Atlantic Fleet was H.S.H. Prince Louis of Battenburg.

This naval visit was naturally the star attraction, not only did the Lord Mayor of London come down but the Japanese royal family, the Chinese ambassador and members of the Turkish parliament all assembled on the pier to look over these mighty ships of war. During the comings and goings of distinguished visitors the curiosity of the crowds blocked the entrance to the pier which was flooded with spectators. So several times it had to be closed in spite of the arrangements previously made, to accommodate and safeguard the public wishing to look at the fleet from the end of the pier.

Those lucky enough to see these warships would have been moved, not only by their armament but the illustrious names they carried. "The Lord Nelson" immortalising the man who over one hundred years' before had commanded

Opposite:
'An Arctic Scene' at Southend-on-Sea, January 16th, 1905. Pictures that tell their own story.

Home and Atlantic Fleets off Southend, July 1909 (Leigh in foreground).

a naval force at the Nore known as "Squadron on Particular Service". There too was the "Temeraire", the modern version of Turner's famous painting which lives on, for

In England's song forever
She's the fighting Temeraire. [1]

This picture was said to be the most luminous of all the works by this famous artist, who had been attracted to the district by reason of its brilliant sunsets. The warship drawing the majority of spectators because of its size, was the first giant battleship, the mighty "Dreadnought", able in spite of its huge armoury, to attain high speeds. The list of these vessels like their history, in those days when Britain ruled the

Naval decorations, Royal Hotel, Southend-on-Sea, July 1909

waves was a remarkable one, and everyone in that holiday atmosphere made known their feeling for them.

Crews were entertained by the local mayor at Southend's show place of "Porters". There were concerts on the pier and wrestling matches, shops were decorated as well as the streets. There were firework displays on either side of the pier, while the fleets were illuminated. Over 1,000 seamen travelled to London and marched to the Guildhall under the command of a Captain Beatty, who was to achieve distinction in World War One, like many of the vessels then laying off the town.

When the eight days' visit came to an end the fleets steamed away, while Admiral May signalled his thanks for the hospitality extended to his command. Then the pier and surroundings were tidied up and the town took some time to recover from the descent from London of 10,000 cyclists in a single day.

Just before the outbreak of World War One, the Third Battle Squadron of the Home Fleet visited the estuary and anchored off the pier, as if to assure people that there was nothing to fear in any confrontation. From Southend the fleet went to Portsmouth and took up its battle station. The river still had its steamboats, while the threat of invasion had been considered but not very seriously, the most likely landing place was thought to be the large field used for kite flying on the northern boundary of the town. Later it was used as an airport although not very effectively by the Royal Flying Corps for Training and Fighter Defence.

This area had once been part of the estates of Rochford Hall, where the amorous Henry VIII had courted the ambitious Ann Boleyn and whose father took his title from the small market town, "Sometimes called the half hundred court" [2] which was bestowed on him by the grateful King. A golf course now borders the busy airport while the historic hall serves as a club house.

The first flight from here was on 31st May, 1915, when a Bleriot airplane took off to intercept a zeppelin, reaching 6,000 feet but the pilot was forced to land at Leigh owing to engine failure. In the same month there was a raid by another airship which dropped a number of incendiary bombs, according to the Germans on "the fortified place of Southend at the estuary of the Thames." [3]

As a result of this and other "intrusions" the irate Southenders had a protest meeting when anti-German feeling ran high, ending with some smashed shop windows owned by those who were thought to be in any way sympathetic to the enemy. People did not feel so badly when the next zeppelin to be in the area was shot down, finishing up 500 yards east of the pier. There were other attacks, the most serious in August 1917, when a number of aircraft unloaded their bombs which resulted in thirty five being killed.

Not many weeks after this, one of our planes landed on the pier doing slight damage to a handrail. The piermaster reported the fact to the committee and that he had written to the commanding officer of the pilot's unit, informing him that an account for the damage done would be sent when estimated. This action can be appreciated when realising how income had suffered as a result of the terrible war then raging just across the water, for although the pier was always open it was utilised mainly by survivors of the devastation.

Queen Mary and her daughter, Princess Mary visited the Royal Naval Hospital named after her on the hill overlooking the pier on June 16th, 1915.

The Palace Hotel overlooking the pier entrance had been used as a naval hospital at the outset of war and re-named after Queen Mary, who visited it in the following June. With their country first invaded it was not surprising that the early casualties were a number of Belgians, who, it is good to record, were allowed free admission to the pier, although this concession was not extended to the nursing staff.

One source of income was obtained from the military authorities when German prisoners and civilians used the pier en route for the ships in the estuary, where they were held in custody. The Admiralty also paid for the war signal station at the pierhead and in October, 1914, a letter from Whitehall requested that the hut used be railed off to keep the public at bay. The piermaster seems to have had other problems concerning servicemen. A letter in January, 1915, dealt with the members of the 8th (Cyclist) Battalion, the Essex Regiment, some of whom he complained had been riding their machines along the pier at excessive speeds, while on despatch duty.

Local firemen were also engaged here, but it seems that their first priority was not fire and attendant hazards, but as ambulance men, in spite of the fact that the pier was vulnerable even then. The appropriate committee authorised the purchase of four stretchers, ambulance hamper and necessary dressings. Fire seems to have been farthest from official minds, for an attempt had been made in the early days of the war to interest the council in a patent fire extinguisher for use on pier properties which included lock-up shops. Even in the days of the local board there was a public outcry at the lack of fire-fighting facilities and when the brigade came into being a fire engine was bought but at first there was nowhere to keep it. The chief constable of Essex said there was no room for it at the police station in Alexandra Road and suggested that application be made to build an engine house at the station.

Showing the hotel in relation to the pier; when it was known as the metropole in 1904, when built.

An effort was made to obtain a coach house in Royal Mews but the sum of four shillings weekly was thought exorbitant. Then a store for the engine in Market Place was recommended but someone made off with the engine. It turned up again and was kept there, in what became the engine room for many years. Twenty years later it was still in the Market Place, because when the firemen were at their annual dinner at the Ship Hotel, a call was received to Southchurch Hall. The men had to run along Marine Parade and up Pier Hill to the engine room and must have been exhausted by the time they reached the scene of the fire.

In spite of many such difficulties the brigade was formed on 2nd October 1877, and only three weeks later in trying out their fire drill, there began a frantic search for water; first they tried the cricket ground, then around Prittlewell, having no luck until finding a supply at the junction of Runwell and Devereux Terraces. Since that early and disastrous beginning the brigade have won numerous prizes in national competitions, since December 1934, under the guidance of the late Captain Percy G. Garon, M.C., "born fireman and fire-fighter,"[4] who won the George Medal dealing with a Thames-side inferno during World War Two.

Southend's Mayor, Alderman J.R. Brightwell, 1894-5, sitting in the mayoral chair made from the oak of the old wooden pier in 1892. (The 'poem' opposite was addressed to this Mayor, who owned the draper's shop, next to the Royal Hotel).

Another person connected with the town for many years was Adam Seebold, conductor of the band and part of the furniture it seemed, of the pier. He started playing there before World War One and performed on after it, right up to the beginning of World War Two. In 1914 there was a proviso that if necessary he would abandon his music but luckily he was able to carry on uninterrupted through enemy action. In the summer months of 1915, his band of twenty two received £50 weekly. During this time Princess Clementine of the Belgians paid a visit to Chalkwell Park on behalf of the Red Cross and her own beleaguered country, and was entertained by the band of the Royal Garrison Artillery. Mr. Seebold's band played on the cliffs but the spotlight was on the army band which often entertained the royal family, and there was a Trumpet Major Laing in it who was called affectionately by Queen Victoria, "my little trumpeter". Within sight and sound of the bandstand where military bands played since the early years of this century, there is a statue of this great queen, looking over the river on which sailed and steamed the ships carrying the intrepid seamen, who helped to create the mighty British Empire over which she ruled.

With the formulation of the municipal borough in 1892, steps were taken to provide entertainment on the pier which was not difficult in such an ideal setting. It was many years before the band was allowed to play on Sunday mornings except after the hours of divine service. This disappointed many people, particularly those who had only that day free from work and so they argued that it was all right to sell cockles and shrimps, apples and oranges, get drunk and fall about the sands but to break the Sabbath listening to the sweet strains of a good band was strictly taboo.

Another bone of contention was the failure to grant a liquor licence, for those who made the long walk on a hot summer's day and reaching the other end found it "dry" and cursed the fact that they carried no flask. Many waxed poetical in the hope that it would soften the hard hearts of the council. There was an appeal to the mayor, who sat in the mayoral chair made from the oak of the original wooden pier:

> *Look down upon us from thy oaken throne*
> *And deign to cast thine eye along the pier,*
> *Man cannot live on Kop's ale alone*
> *He wants sometimes a little drop of beer.* [5]

To cater for the holidaymakers who still came to the town, public houses, in the first half of the war, were open all day, so that anyone wishing to slake their thirst could do so, without going on the pier, where a member of the Essex constabulary was on duty. When the county borough was formed the Southend Borough Constabulary came into being on April 1st, 1914. The headquarters of the local force was in Alexandra Street and when the initial inspection of the police in their smart new uniforms took place, the council members seemed well pleased at the appearance of the newly-formed body, for their outfits had cost only £3 each. Then it was learnt that the splendid uniform worn by the freshly appointed chief constable, Mr. Henry Maurice Kerslake, had been valued at £45; there were gasps of disbelief, resulting in Councillor Bradley — the old pierhead master — suggesting that a charge should be made for the public to view it. [6]

Still, even Captain, later Admiral McHardy, chief constable of the Essex Constabulary, had his problems when the force was formed in 1840. He had no proper office and had to make do with a room in the gaol at Springfield — surely the only chief of police starting his appointment in prison premises. The act for the formation of the Metropolitan Police had received the royal assent, in the same year as the pier bill, and took control of the Thames river police, the co-founder of which had been John Harriott, who lived at "Broomhills", Great Stambridge.

During the war there were several thousand servicemen stationed in the area but they caused little trouble to the police, being like the majority of people of that period, less demonstrative, but more disciplined in their attitude. So it seemed whenever punishment was meted out it was always a harsh sentence for rather minor offences, as if the magistrates were quite overcome that it was at all necessary to commit a crime.

The pier committee dealt with what was referred to them as "the promiscuous collection of shellfish from the shore". The piermaster stated that he had taken precautions to prevent any unlawful removal from the seashore and the cost of "watching" he estimated at £200 yearly. This seemed to be effective, for it was reported to the committee that a person was charged with stealing shellfish from the front belonging to the corporation, and he was given three months' imprisonment with hard labour.

While the police were not directly involved in this case they were very necessary when fatal accidents took place. One occurred when a small boy disregarding the warnings of his mother fell on to the electric tramway. So poor, so distraught, she asked for a small grant for funeral expenses. And help was given. A month later, in August 1917, a lady swimming from a bathing machine was drowned. The owner had his licence withdrawn because he had no boat ready for launching in such an emergency.

In the last year of the war, holiday crowds reflected the tense atmosphere then prevailing and fewer people came to the town as the Germans launched their last great offensive. Then there was a great boost to morale when the story was told of an ordinary, insignificant ferry boat working on the Mersey being chosen with another boat to land raiding parties at Zeebruge. The British forces were suffering heavy losses from attacks by enemy submarines and the Daffodil, as she was then called, set out on the night of 22nd April, 1918, to assist HMS Vindictive put the submarine base at Bruges out of action by blocking the canal.

The raid was entirely successful, the one-time ferry boat keeping the warship alongside the Mole by driving her stern hard against the Vindictive, allowing men to be landed to carry out their mission of destruction. As the result of her work on this St. George's Day, the king ordered that in future she be known as the "Royal Daffodil", a name that was to become familiar with all those making trips on the river. Some twenty years after, she returned to the Belgian coast where her adventures had earned royal and national recognition and was broken up. In 1939, another steamboat of the same name followed in the wake of the first, being built on the Clyde like many others. She was the only two-funnelled pleasure craft designed for continental trips, and came safely through World War Two after being engaged for most of the time on trooping.

By this time ships were able to communicate by wireless telegraphy, which had been invented by Marconi and used at the time of the Boer War as an experiment. During this period the inventor opened up a factory at Chelmsford and a demonstration in this new fangled method of signalling was conducted at the pavilion on the pier in 1900, by Lloyds, Trinity House and the Board of Trade.

Since 1883, there has been a signal station at the pierhead where the movement of ships were recorded by Lloyd's of London. There were several requests for more room as this business increased and near the end of World War One the navy were allowed to erect a wireless station on top of the old refreshment rooms, after a naval officer had attended personally at a meeting of the pier committee to complain that because of piles and rafters the men were unable to discern names of passing ships. When the war was over the Admiralty wrote expressing their appreciation of the help given by the corporation and stating that the signal station, as requested be transferred to the council for the agreed sum of £50.

Before war ended Southend began its tradition as the "Guiness Pocket Borough" with the election of Captain the Hon. Rupert Guiness as Member of Parliament for the county borough. When he became Lord Iveagh on the death of his father, his wife, the Countess of Iveagh, took over the seat until 1935. Daughter of the Earl of Onslow, she was the twenty-second member of her family to sit in Parliament. Her son-in-law, Henry "Chips" Channon succeeded her and when the borough was divided into two constituencies, he chose Southend, West. Friend of royalty and West End host, he was knighted in 1957, the year before he died. His son, Paul Channon, carries on the family's service to the community, while Southend, East, is represented by Sir Stephen McAdden, C.B.E., both belonging to the Conservative Party.

FOOTNOTES

1. Quoted Thames Estuary by William Addison. p 13.chl.
   (picture of the Fighting Temeraire was painted in 1839)
2. The history of Rochford Hundred by P. Benton. vol 2 p.782. 1886
3. The Southend Standard. 7th June, 1915.
4. Southend-on-Sea Fire Brigade compiled by H.O. Crompton. 1877-1937.p.5.
5. Remarks. 25th May, 1895.
6. Southend-on-Sea County Borough Constabulary by Williams and Doxsey. p.5.ch 1

Chapter Ten

Southenders had plenty to do and see during the Armistice Day celebrations which followed the downfall of the Kaiser, although there were many families affected by the war, who had nothing to celebrate. Those who had, witnessed the German merchant ships moored in the estuary in accordance with the Armistice agreement. These arrived on 25th March 1919, staying for two weeks.

Soon afterwards the battle squadrons of the Home Fleet and the battle cruiser of the Atlantic Fleet lay off Southend and on the day designated as "Peace Day" fired a salute. The local bonfire committee, formed to get the illuminations going, wanted to burn an old sand barge lying on the beach but were stopped in their tracks, when officially informed that the timber of the hulk was valued at £40. While understanding the enthusiasm of the people in victory, the realities had to be faced and poverty and unemployment were very much in evidence.

The local War Pensions committees urged the employment of disabled servicemen on the pier, and at least one ex-soldier was taken on as a tram driver, but when two trams

The Home Fleet and part of the Atlantic Fleet fired a salute on 'Peace Day' as they lay off Southend, marking the end of World War One.

collided he was blamed for the accident, losing the bonus paid for accident-free periods, and put on other work. Later the enemy submarine, Deutschland, was placed on exhibition at the pierhead to help raise money for King George's fund for sailors. This was organised by the late Horatio Bottomley, editor of *John Bull* and Member of Parliament, who was later imprisoned for fraud and expelled from the Commons.

Before and after the war there were several hare-brained schemes put to the council, especially that regarding the pier and its approaches, one taken seriously was that launched by a local body calling itself the Westcliff Tradesmen's Association, which applied for permission to erect a pier a mile away from the original. The advent of war turned men's minds to more serious things but it had been triggered off by a report in a national paper that the town was to have another pier several years previously. This was not altogether surprising considering how well the one in operation was doing and was a great compliment to it.

Plans were, it said, in process of being drawn up by a London syndicate for a £400,000 structure on the Western Esplanade and was to include a Lido swimming pool, sunshine lounges, concert hall, amusement deck, and children's boating and bathing pools. A start was supposed to be made on the project in the following year — 1903 — and was to be 800 yards long and 80 feet wide. It was expected to take two years to complete, and, most important

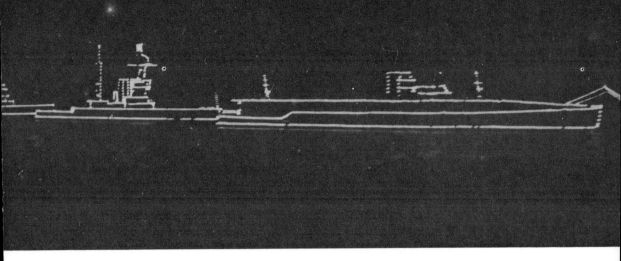

of all, was to employ 2,500 workers.

Sometime elapsed before another shot was fired. This time it came from a different group with the same ideas, having the more imposing title of the Chalkwell Hall Trust Ltd. At a meeting, the company asked if there was any prospect of proceeding with the building of a Westcliff pier. If not, the company would exercise their "right" to carry out the work. The council re-affirmed their intention to do nothing at all, which seemed obvious from the beginning.

The applicants threatened to get on with it themselves but the only action that the syndicate took was to arrange an exhibition of their plans of the proposed building on the Westcliff jetty.

Then a Mr. Hart appeared and he submitted "an entirely new proposal" for the erection of a short pleasure pier upon the foreshore east of Grosvenor Road, Westcliff. He had been making an attempt to obtain a portion of the pier which he had wanted to let, now he had turned to this more ambitious scheme which entailed a large ballroom, concert hall, and high class refreshment rooms, similar in character to the pleasure piers at Brighton, Bournemouth and other resorts.

The committee were favourably impressed and thought that a suitably designed pier up to 1,000 feet long and 100 feet wide with properly constructed buildings for the public, coupled with good orchestral performances and concert

Exhibition of plans for a proposed pier at Westcliff, 5th January, 1912 (Can you see the ghostly figure?)

parties, being available for residents and visitors alike, would add to the attractions of the borough as a whole. Mr. Hart was asked by letter whether he would be willing to grant the corporation an option to acquire this building at anytime after erection if they desired to do so. There is no record of any reply.

At a joint meeting of the committees of pier, parks and entertainments departments on 25th October 1921, the borough surveyor asked that the desirability of transferring the pavilion on the pier to a selected position on the cliffs, should be considered. This surely was the start of the movement resulting after many delays in building the present Cliffs Pavilion at Shorefields.

The prize applicant seems to have been a Mr. H.J. Monson, in terms of the number of schemes he proposed to carry out for the mutual benefit of himself and the corporation. He asked permission to remove mud from the foreshore for medicinal purposes, with a view to the establishment of a hydro in the town. Every facility was given him to take samples as required. Before long he was giving a glowing account of the samples he had taken, which according to his analysis showed that they "contained radio active properties and by virtue of its powerful energising emanation has valuable curative powers; also that persons suffering from rheumatism, neuritis, and similar maladies, would derive considerable benefit from a course of treatment in which the mud was properly used."

Fired by his enthusiasm it was only to be expected that he was given the go-ahead to take what he wanted, in the way of mud, for a period of three years. Mr. Monson was back again before long, asking to be allowed to take five tons daily for the same reasons. The town clerk, regarding this as rather a tall order, said that sanction of the Port of London Authority would be necessary. This was granted on condition that the mud was treated locally and the name of Southend-on-Sea identified with any projects used for commercial purposes.

Mr. Monson then asked to be allowed to moor his houseboat on the seafront, west of the Bell wharf and permission for a 70 foot long structure was sought on the foreshore, on the west side of the Leigh bathing station, so that he could give treatment by mud bath and at an adjoining kiosk, sell radio active oil; explaining to the public at the same time, the method which he employed. The applicant was told that the railway company claimed jurisdiction over the sea wall and their permission would be necessary. Also present at this meeting were some irate ratepayers from Leigh who asked the corporation not to allow any boat or structure for use as club premises, to be placed on the foreshore at Leigh. In view of these objections the applicant seemed to have lost the day, for there were no more requests from him.

The council sanctioned this water chute in 1902, but the venture failed. Afterwards it became a boating pool and in more recent times, 'home' of the Golden Hind, flagship of Francis Drake, modelled on the original ship in which he brought home Spanish booty and a great deal of glory.

The chute having been removed, it became a boating pool.

There seemed to have been a surplus of aircraft after World War One, to judge from the spate of applications from aviation companies who wanted the sole right of plying for hire from the pier or beach, while a Gotha biplane was offered to the town on behalf of the Air Ministry, subject to the council making arrangements to house it. The gift was accepted and it was placed in the sunken gardens. Messrs. Short Bros. outlined their plans for a service of seaplanes, while another concern wanted to hire out four seater biplanes and permission to erect a hangar.

Rough water in what later became the boating pool, looking from the east towards the pier.

An offer was made to provide seaplanes complete with
pilot and mechanics, while another planned to use a place
off the beach where they could move their planes at night
by means of a small wheeled carriage to transport them.
In the following year the company who had been successful
built a hangar on Shoebury Common, off which buoys were
laid down when Trinity House gave sanction.

The Duke of York, then Prince Albert, later George VI,
came to Southend on 14th July 1920, and opened the beautiful grounds of Priory Park, which had been given to the town
by one of the most generous of men; Mr. R.A. Jones, M.B.E.,
respected family jeweller of the High Street, Southend. In
this park mayoral garden parties were held near the old
priory, where the Cluniac monks had their cloister until
the dissolution of the monasteries. Not only did Mr. Jones
give this but also the memorial ground named after him in
1914, in memory of his wife, for the use of children. Then
the final gesture of generosity was his gift of Victory sports
ground, as a memorial to local sportsmen killed in World War
One.

On his visit the future king also opened the Naval and Military club at the end of Royal Terrace, nearly opposite to the spot where the flag of the Alexandra yacht club flies, inviting attention to the oldest institution of its kind in the district. Founded in 1873, it was the nerve centre of a yacht race four years later, when the course went around the English coastline, starting and finishing at the pier.

George V came the year after his son to participate in the local Yachting Week. A lot of work was required behind the scenes for the commander of the royal yacht inquired regarding the provision of suitable moorings near the pier. The piermaster had to obtain a loan of these from Sheerness, and the king's harbour master came to inspect the arrangements made for the Victoria and Albert and escort of war vessels.

Yachting week was from the 11th to the 16th July, and during this period no fishing was allowed on the pier. The sum of £50 was also allocated to the piermaster for illuminations. The king's assistant private secretary wrote to the mayor stating the king would pay a private visit to the borough on the 14th July, to embark on the Victoria and Albert moored off the pier extension. Travelling down by what was then the Great Eastern Railway, he would be proceeding by car from the station using the tramway to reach the extension.

All this was very good publicity for the town and was repeated in 1923 the formula being practically the same, with the harbour master and the Admiralty combining with the royal staff to make sure that everything was in order. The piermaster was able to spend money on decorations, after putting up the "no fishing" signs again.

Very much in the public eye at this time were the local yacht clubs who helped to organise this one special event every year. Also evident at this time was the pilfering that occurred to craft moored on the foreshore, causing the clubs to ask for someone with police powers to be employed to stop the theft and damage. Eventually the pier committee sanctioned an additional foreshore inspector for this purpose, the yachtsmen having promised that they would consider paying half the cost of his employment.

At the same meeting the five yacht clubs in the borough, through a representative, asked if the committee would consider constructing a hardway on the foreshore, from the vicinity of the Crowstone in south easterly direction to low water, to enable all boat owners to board and disembark from their craft at all states of the tide. Full details of plans and costing were required. An experimental section of hard-

Showing the Tollhouse and horses ready for hire. c1905. (They were called 'Bell horses' and pulled carts up the hill).

way was laid, which withstood all storms and tide movements during the winter. So another matter was resolved.

During the yachting weeks of 1925-6, there was no royal visit but in spite of this — perhaps because of it — clubs kept the committee on their toes by one or two requests, which would have done credit to the king's harbour master. They asked for the provision of a mark boat in support of the laying down of moorings in the vicinity of the pierhead, and the marking of the entrance to the Ray by small fairway buoys. There were no objections by the Port of London Authority, but proposals were submitted to the elder brethren of Trinity House for marking the entrance to the Ray by small can buoys on port hand and conical buoys on starboard hand. Mark spars were erected on the foreshore west of the pier, approximately a mile south and parallel with the beach to indicate the measured mile. Trinity House raised no objections.

The old hero of many rescues at sea, William Bradley, was in June 1922, sitting as an alderman and a member of the pier committee, when the action of another pierhead keeper — Mr. E.J. Cotgrove — was brought forward as the gallant rescuer of two girls in serious danger of drowning; having lost their rowing boat, they were clinging to the piles on the old pierhead. He was commended for his prompt action and on the suggestion that one guinea should be awarded, the mayor stated that he would have pleasure in presenting as a personal gift this sum as a token of his appreciation. The name of Cotgrove is a familiar one in the early history of the borough. At one of the first meetings of the pier committee a Mr. Cotgrove made application for ground space on the beach or on the hill, which ever was available, suggesting that he could place automatic machines on the pier and approaches. He must have been a far-sighted man for this appears to have been the first mention of these machines which later came under the control of a Mr. Arnold.

There had been so many life saving acts, often at great peril to the rescuer, that it was decided that a special medal should be struck and presented called the pier life saving medal. This was decided on the 23rd December 1926, and the first recipient was of course Mr. E.J. Cotgrove! He was a four times winner, stretching from 1914 to 1922, only second in spite of that to a Mr. W.J. Lilley, who had made five rescues, covering the period from 1895 to 25th October 1910. During the next few years there were many other names to add to the roll of rescuers: Messrs Cundy, Clemensha, Webster, Purbrick, Brand, Myall, Stanley, Miss Ansell and Captain Flett.

Before the rush to the sea began. A view from Pier Hill looking down on the boats in the river and horse and cart ready for action.

As a result of the presentation of the pier life saving medal, a complaint was received from the local Chamber of Trade regarding the fact that they were obtained from a firm outside the borough without first obtaining tenders from local traders. The town clerk stated that special dies had to be prepared by die sinkers, and the committee were not aware that any firm in the district undertook such work. Whether this reply satisfied the businessmen is not known, but the reason prompting the inquiry can be understood, for there was still a great deal of poverty in the area, where unemployment was not just a winter hazard. It was only natural that the pier, being a thriving industry should help to alleviate some of the unemployment and resultant poverty.

This was done and there are many local traders who have been sustained by orders for materials placed by the pier undertaking. With the progress made and the repairs required,

The view from Pier Hill, with the Concert Hall Stand on the right, with a show in progress.

building items have often been ordered and the same applies to the purchase of coal, towels and bathing costumes, chairs and clocks. Some of the unemployed who were often the poor ex-servicemen, were used on scraping the barnacles from the pier piles at eleven pence, and a farthing for an hour's work, which stopped the erosion of the protective tar around the piles, but did little to protect the man.

As late as November 1930, it was officially recognised that unemployment was much too common, especially

A view of the pier from the west side, showing motor vehicles which would be worth a fortune today!

among those who fought in the war to end all wars. A circular from the King's National Roll Council asked the corporation that they only employ as contractors those firms enrolled with the council, so as to reduce the number of disabled ex-servicemen. There had been a letter too from the Chamber of Shipping of the United Kingdom, regarding the government's proposals for the relief of unemployment by the development of ports and harbours. It was about this time, as the country slowly recovered from the effects of World War One that it was decided to do something about the old tollhouse at the pier entrance. A scheme was planned to remove it and widen the pier on the west side over the Sunken Garden, from Pier Hill to approximately 160 yards south of the Pavilion. There were also plans for the provision of a new theatre or winter garden for 2,000, with the inclusion of a bandstand which was going to be removed from the end of the pier, and the conversion of the Pavilion into

Showing the popularity of the pier by the crowds leaving it. c1910.

This was the old Palladium Theatre at the pier entrance, 7th September 1920.

a dance hall. Under the widened structure an extensive arcade with shops was proposed, affording large shelter accommodation. The estimated cost was £250,000.

The wind of change seemed to have been very slow in blowing in this direction, for the old tollhouse was not removed until 1931, and the council did not seem to know where to put the new pavilion. In the previous year it was suggested the Sunken Garden would be a good place for it, with an escalator operating from Royal Terrace to Western Esplanade. It seemed the Pier Hill concert hall was to be removed to make way for offices for the piermaster and staff, including the widening of the west side and new pier entrance. This was to be built over the roadway of the esplanade to relieve the congestion of pedestrian traffic. As we know today, part of this scheme was carried out eventually. The piermaster had his offices and a new entrance was constructed, but the escalator did not get beyond the drawing board.

This Concert Hall Stand cum Bandstand was removed 1930/1 with the old Tollhouse.

Southend-on-Sea Lifeboats – 100 Years of Service

Boys of England & Edwin J. Brett 1879-1887

Theodore and Herbert 1887-1899

James Stevens 1900-1927

Greater London 1928-1955

Greater London 1955-1976

Percy Garon 1976

Chapter Eleven

There was nothing new in advertising, as local newspapers had carried the formal type from their inception and could not very well exist without them, but through the L.M.S. Railway, the corporation were given the opportunity in February, 1929, of exhibiting a scale model of the pier and seafront. The firm was Messrs. Lewis of Birmingham, who offered window space for this purpose in connection with their display of holiday requirements. The piermaster duly produced a model, and as it was required for the firm's stores in Liverpool and Manchester as well; he was asked for two more. Not to be outdone, Messrs. John Walsh Ltd., of Sheffield, wrote offering to display free of charge, a model of the same pier and seafront, six feet by seven feet, with accompanying posters.

Southend was getting a lot of publicity through the steamship companies who had 100,000 copies of their "Holiday Express" issued each summer in the metropolitan area, giving a list of hotels etc. in the Southend and Thanet regions. It was thought, to go with this, that a friendly, illuminated sign on the roof of the pavilion "Welcome to our Visitors" would be an appropriate greeting. The suggestion was turned down because of the expense involved.

In spite of this, business seemed to be exceptional, for the piermaster reported that on Sunday, 15th July, 1928, there were more visitors than at any other Sunday in the history of the undertaking. The figures being: admissions 31,280, number of passengers landing and embarking 16,547. Perhaps because of this Mr. R. Arnold, licensee of the automatic machines, had to appear before the pier committee because of complaints that his machines had broken down. He produced by way of answer, a large quantity of discs and base metal coins which were the cause of the complaint. Even the piermaster suffered in this respect, but he was reimbursed.

Through the L.M.S. Railway, the owners of the Tilbury to Dunkirk service queried the depth of water needed to permit the passage of their steamers of between 1,500-2,000 tons, as the question of a service to Southend was being considered. Although the depth of water was said to be sufficient, scale models of the steamboats were obtained and as a result fender piles were increased in length, three to four feet above the deck level. The marine superintendent of the shipping company inspected the pierhead and found the arrangements were satisfactory.

This meant that in fog or other adverse weather the pier was able to receive passengers who would otherwise have gone on to Tilbury. It also catered for the landing of perishable goods, such as flowers and vegetables, all of which would be taken by special train to London. Sir John Francis, a member of the pier committee, visited the Home Office and in consequence facilities were provided for H.M. Customs and the Aliens' Branch, and company's stevedores. From May, 1930, several emergency calls were made, and the L.M.S. Railway expressed thanks for the work carried out in this respect.

It was a blow when, after two years, this service was transferred to Folkestone, especially as so much had been done to cater for the requirements of the A.L.A. company. (Angleterre-Lorraine-Alsace).

By this time the eastern arm of the pier extension was finished and in May, 1929, as Prince George, Duke of Kent, had agreed to perform the opening ceremony of the new Southend lifeboat. On a date in July, arranged by the Royal National Lifeboat Institution, it was decided to invite H.R.H. to open the extension at the pierhead. This was agreed, so that on 7th July Prince George launched the "Greater London" lifeboat from the slipway belonging to the Alexandra yacht club, on the west side of the pier. He then went on to open the extension named after him.

Looking back it seems strange that the local lifeboat

The Southend Lifeboat 'Greater London,' stationed at the Pier Head did great war service. It was launched on 66 occasions, rescued and landed over 300—crews of various ships. It assisted in saving 28 ships of various sizes and went to Dover to help in saving our troops at Dunkirk.

then had no station on the pier. The very first boat "The Boys of England and Edwin J. Brett" was obtained in 1879, being paid for by a special fund through a magazine which gave its name to the town's first lifeboat. Its boathouse was at the corner of Seaway and Hartington Road, just off the seafront at Marine Parade, being pulled there on rollers from the water. Since those days the lifeboat service has in the finest traditions of its calling rescued about 1,100 lives. It has progressed from rowing, to sailing, to motor boat, although its crew are volunteers, who in their dedication used to run down the pier when the alarm was sounded, before the electric trains came into being.

It was in July 1932, that the Royal National Lifeboat Institution made known its desire for the erection of a lifeboat station with committee room, etc., in its present position on the pier. For this purpose the Board of Trade was asked if it was willing to convey to the corporation the tidal lands making up the proposed site. There was no problem here and a lease was granted, subject to the conditions laid down by the Port of London Authority.

Five months' later the R.N.L.I. asked if this work could start without delay and were informed that this would be in order when the council's licence had been sealed. Soon afterwards the institution were told that work could start on payment of £1 weekly when the piermaster would issue passes for the men shortly to be employed. The station was eventually opened by Lord Ritchie of Dundee, chairman of the P.L.A. in July, 1935, when the pier was a holiday resort in itself. Now times have changed but the weather and the sea can be just as treacherous, and there is concern that pier workers who now man the boat may lose their jobs; so men may lose their lives at sea. For according to Councillor Beryl Schofield, the lifeboat was launched fifty-seven times last year (1978) and sixty-four lives were saved.[1] This lady has frequently championed the cause of the pier in the council chamber and earned the gratitude of numerous Southenders, who like her, regard the pier as part of our heritage. Christine Ronan and John Hodgkins of the "Save the Pier Committee" are others dedicated to the same cause.

It is not just a question of saving lives that earned lifeboatmen their enviable reputation, when putting out to sea in any kind of weather, although it is naturally their primary consideration. For even a storm-driven crewless vessel was enough to send them out on an early November morning in 1921. A Dutch boat collided with the pier destroying cast iron piles, and the lifeboatmen removed and re-moored it during a hurricane to a safer position near the old pierhead.

This damage was caused by the Thames conservancy hulk 'Marlborough' on 23rd November, 1908 Soon afterwards luminous paint was used on the pier and a motor vessel patrolled in the vicinity on the approach of stormy weather, to make sure all boats were properly moored.

Because of its length and the ships moored in the vicinity gale force winds and rough seas have always been a source of anxiety to those serving on the pier. One of the worst disasters already mentioned, was on the old wooden pier when it was sliced in two by a barge belonging to the embarassed George Vandervord, who had been chairman of the local board for five years; for the pierhead keeper was stranded on the end, while his family had to be rescued from their house on the pierhead. This was not unlike the accident which occurred at Margate on 24th November 1877, when "a storm driven wreck sliced the pier marooning between forty to fifty people at the seaward end, who were not rescued until the following day."[1a]

At Southend, the next serious event was fourteen years on when a lighter hit the pier putting it out of action for some days. Then on 10th December, 1898, a ketch went right through the structure, doing over £1,000 of damage. The next trespasser was a hay-laden barge, which on 7th December, 1907, caused sixty feet of decking to be replaced, and in the following year the hulk Marlborough also destroyed the same amount of timber, and the hulk was swept out as far as the Nore lightship.

Even more serious was the destruction wreaked by the concrete motor ship Violette which made a gap of 180 feet and after the impact the vessel sank on the west side, settling down over a number of broken piles. As a result the erection of a temporary passing point on the pier had to be built, while a Westminster firm undertook the repairs, for the large sum in those days, of £5,554.

It was the piermaster's correspondence with Trinity House that resulted in warning notices to mariners of the unsafe mooring near the accident prone pier. Another safety precaution was the insertion of red glass in the pier lamps, which were kept alight at night during the winter months. As in all cases of lighting the sanction of Trinity House was obtained, while the P.L.A. and the Board of Trade were kept informed of everything appertaining to the installation of safety measures.

There were many instances when such notices were necessary. Even when the electric siren at the eastern end of the Prince George extension was installed, for use during foggy weather, when steamers were expected, it was officially considered that at least one month's notice of the installation should be given to mariners.

One thing is certain in all this, the piermaster Captain J.C. Johnson, ran the pier in true naval tradition, so that when the Home Fleet lay between the pier and the Nore in May 1935, in celebration of the king's Silver Jubilee, Commander-in-Chief, Admiral the Earl of Cork and Orrery, K.C.B., was greatly impressed by the smooth running of the pier. This caused him to write in appreciation: "You and your staff have afforded every possible facility and consideration to the officers and men of the fleet." Through his secretary he spoke of the courtesy and attention, handling and control of boat and pedestrian traffic, and stating that "the pier was a model of efficient organisation."[2]

There was no talk then of recession. In the middle 1930s the climax of Southend's season came when the

Another view of the damaged pier.

illuminations were switched on transforming the seafront and pier into a fairyland of light which attracted nearly two million visitors from all over Britain and Europe. There were more than one hundred set pieces on the pier alone, reaching out to the river where the famous old steamboats tied up most days. Scintillating overhead strip lighting, illuminated pylons, flashing arrows and twinkling stars led the way to the Kursaal, or for the children, where their dreams were realised in the enchanting "Never Never Land". In contrast the cliffs presented a quiet, enchanted garden,

The cost of this 'collision' was over £5,000, when the concrete ship 'Violette' hit the pier, so that a temporary passing point had to be put down (January 1921).

with trees, shrubberies and rockeries picked out by coloured floodlights, and relieved here and there by illuminated floral designs of an assortment of exotic birds and lanterns.

It was not only the lights that drew the visitor to the borough. There were the Yachting, Carnival and cricket weeks that attracted their quota of holidaymakers. Most popular event, which grew gradually from a weak one-day effort in the mid 1920s was the carnival, drawing entrants from all over the country and large crowds to watch the parades and processions. As a result of generous donations in the early days and land given by the Earl of Iveagh, the Duchess of York, now the Queen Mother, had laid the foundation-stone of the General Hospital. Another royal visitor was Prince Henry, who had opened the London-Southend Arterial Road three years previously.

At a pier committee meeting on the 20th December, 1934, the town clerk submitted extracts from newspapers published between 1829-1837, containing references to the building of the original pier. The piermaster later produced a copy of admiralty charts of the estuary published in 1835, which was the first date that the pier had been recognised. As a result of this evidence, immediate steps seemed to have been taken to arrange the centenary of the pier in July 1935, although the foundation-stone had been laid and the building commenced in July 1929, the first portion being ready to receive the public in the following year.

Celebrations and special events were arranged to take place from July 24 to 31, including the official opening of the lifeboat house already mentioned. Special dances and concerts were to be held on the pier, where the Shoebury-ness garrison band was asked to perform. The committee were almost carried away by their enthusiasm, for they authorised the sale of intoxicating liquor for the pier caterers. This motion was later referred back and lost; so the lines written by one overcome by thirst at the end of the pier, still applied:

O'er the pier white gulls sail lazily by
Thru' the arc of the infinite blue;
Says the warm sweet sun, when the day is done,
There isn't a drink for you.

At last, the dream nurtured in a few local breasts, of building another pier at Westcliff was finally laid to rest, when the pier committee issued a lengthy statement explaining why it was necessary to pay the sum of £4,000, when a local resident surrendered his right to erect such a structure. It arose in 1903, when in the conveyance of the Chalkwell foreshore at Westcliff to the corporation, they became owners of Chalkwell Park and land on the Chalkwell Esplanade, as well as the foreshore, the vendors reserving the right to themselves and their assignees to erect and maintain a pier not exceeding 800 yards long. There was also a covenant in the conveyance that the corporation should not erect or construct on this foreshore any buildings or works without consent of the vendors.

The committee decided that the corporation should have entire control of the foreshore and "the right of private persons to build a pier be terminated." The minutes also

Showing the damage done by a hay-laden barge on the 7th December 1907.

refer to the fact that the consent of the vendors would also be required in connection "with the proposed changes to Bell Wharf at Leigh." It was pointed out that a Mr. F. May had succeeded to the rights of the vendors in the building of a pier and execution of works on the foreshore at Westcliff. Mr. May seemed quite happy to hand over his rights for the sum of £4,000, while the council, too, must have been relieved to bring to an end amicably, a business that had lasted for over thirty years and caused a great deal of agitation to those who controlled the Southend pier.[3]

Another dream, just as fondly nourished, but more practicable in design, was the suggested yacht harbour proposed on the east side of the pier. This matter was discussed on 20th May 1937, and the harbour was planned in the vicinity of the lifeboat station which would accommodate a large number of boats. It was stated that representatives of the inter yacht clubs had approached Sir Alexander Gibb and partners, who had agreed to submit a report to the corporation on what seemed to be a feasible proposition. There was a proviso from the firm that if the scheme was carried out, they would be retained as consulting engineers.

The report on the necessary work was placed before the committee, including dredging operations, and the provision of slipways, landing stages, moorings and premises required for the sale and storage of equipment. Also the possible levy of a small toll on pedestrians using the promenade surrounding the proposed harbour. The pier committee appeared favourably impressed with the whole idea of the harbour which would enhance the reputation of the town as a yachting centre.

Nearly eighteen months later the report and plans

94

submitted by Sir Alexander Gibb was referred to a special sub-committee for consideration. Soon afterwards there were more urgent matters to consider as the war clouds gathered.

It was only a brief announcement by the Watch Committee on the 16th September 1937, which hardly caused the flutter of an eyelid, but reading it now, that notice seems most significant. It was to the effect that Chief Inspector Hawkins and Sergeant Cheatle of the local constabulary, were given authority to train persons in anti-gas measures , both having qualified at the anti-gas school at Falfield.

Later in the year the Nore Command Passive Defence Committee proposed to hold a day and night air raid exercise in the area in November 1937 and again on 31st May, 1938. By this time an Air Raid Precautions Officer had been appointed. Schools were used as A.R.P. posts and perhaps the greatest impression made on the public was the demonstration shelters provided in the main parks of the town; those at Shoebury, Southchurch, Priory, Chalkwell and Belfairs being utilised; for where people enjoyed their leisure in watching or playing a variety of sports, now these pleasure grounds were being associated with a far grimmer prospect.

In the last days of peace — the piermaster submitted a report of government requirements and the licences of certain business presmises were terminated. Even the special concert proposed to mark the termination of Adam Seebold's long association with the entertainment was cancelled. War had a lot to answer for, even before it started.

Pier damaged on 7th December, 1907, when 60 feet of decking had to be replaced.

FOOTNOTES

1. In use since 1976 is a smaller three-manned lifeboat, named after the old fire chief and enthusiastic secretary of the lifeboat — 'Percy Garon'. An electric buggy has now been provided by the R.N.L.I. to get lifeboatmen to the pierhead.
1a. Seaside Piers by Simon H. Adamson (1977) p.40.
2. Letter read to the Pier Committee on 23rd May, 1935.
3. Pier Committee on 6th June, 1935. (Both 2 and 3 Southend Borough Proceedings of the Council and Committees).

Chapter
Twelve

Ever since the time when Hilter's youth started singing their songs of hate and harassment there had been a fear that sooner or later the smouldering flames of such hatred would burst into war, so that when it came a lot had been done to prepare for it. There had been a sense of urgency not present before, for the world had grown so much smaller and the armies poised just across the water were only a short flying distance away.

Southend's pier was called to the colours on August 25th, 1939, becoming H.M.S. Leigh, while the flag of the Thames and Medway Naval Control Service flew from its headquarters on Royal Terrace. By this time a great deal had been accomplished; the Observer Corps had been preparing a year before, at the same time amateur yachtsmen formed an emergency service. Provision for searchlights on the pier had been arranged even before this, while the aerodrome was taken over by the Royal Air Force as an advanced fighter station. It had been used again four years previously as a civil airport, being bought by the Southend corporation. [1]

A few days after the outbreak of the war, while the pier was still opened to the public, the first ever convoy sailed from the end of it. The Admiralty were naturally delighted at the success of this initial enterprise and sent a congratulatory telegram to all involved. This was the beginning of the six years' struggle during which the long nose of the pier was stuck in many naval and military matters.

Seven weeks after the dreaded declaration the Germans made a night-time aerial attack on the river, dropping mag-

netic mines, including one that was later recovered at Shoebury and made history in the process. (2) With the big guns of
the artillery garrison in the east and the R.A.F. station to the
north, the shipping was defended but was always vulnerable
to aerial attack. Yet, never again was it seriously threatened
off the pier, which caused the then Petty Office A.P. Herbert
M.P., to write in his story of those times: "Many a day on
patrol, many an evening from the Palace hotel windows, I
have seen the placid herd of ships off the pier, such a target,
such a prize and wondered why the enemy did not assault
and harry them night and day. After all, the pier was only
65 miles from Calais." (3)   The only explanation is that
London was only just up the river and that was the prime
target.

Where Adam Seebold so often conducted with Jack
Upson at the piano, "there came together more merchant
masters than have ever come together in one place in all the
world." As a result of those conferences over 84,297 ships
left the pierhead in convoy. Many of course were sunk, and
often the survivors would return to their departure point,
coming ashore on the trains built for happy holidaymakers,
now running night and day on the urgent task of ferrying the
sick and wounded of battles fought on every front. This
electric railway now a casualty itself, carried during the
World War Two, over one-and-a-half million servicemen and
women.

There were many problems to be overcome before
vessels sailed in convoy. Usually it was the presence of
mines that caused most delays; on one occasion there was
a hold up of three days, during which time 140 ships congregated. Sometimes the human element was involved as related
by Alan Herbert, when one ship with a Muslim crew refused
to sail because it was a feast day, and according to their
custom on that particular day a sheep had to be sacrificed.
So naval control duly obliged and sent one out to the vessel
by means of a tug called appropriately "The Shepherd Lad".
After the crew had completed their ritual they sailed on
time.

Food to satisfy the majority of palates was supplied at all
hours and the sailor M.P. wrote with gratitude of the catering
manager, who ran the pier cafe with the aid of a cheerful,
willing lady known as "Mona", to the masters of the
merchant navy everywhere.

Then came the call to Dunkirk. Nothing in the whole
history of World War Two was such a disaster to the retreat-
ing armies or such a triumph for those who rescued the
troops from certain annihilation or years of incarceration in

prison camps. When the amazing armada set out to the rescue the British and Allied forces it captured the imagination of the free world, performing what has been called "the greatest small boat achievement in naval history".[4] The rescue force was made up of coasters and colliers, trawlers and tugs, bawleys and barges, pleasure boats, lifeboats and Leigh fishing craft, all steaming down the river to their assembly point, at the beginning of what John Masefield called "the nine days wonder".

As the result of the efforts of those assorted seamen, 335,000 men of the British Expeditionary Forces were saved — saved to fight again. That adventure will always be a source of pride to the seafaring men of the district, for there were the two Skylarks, the two Dreadnoughts, Britannia, Monarch, Queen Alexandra, The Queen, Grey Starling, Prince of Wales, Nemo, Sea Foam, Wild Heather, Canvey Queen, Princess Maud, Duchess of York, another Prince of Wales from Shoebury and Southend's lifeboat. In that array were six bawleys from Leigh, who saved over 1,000 men and lost some of their own, when the Renown was blown up and Frank and Leslie Osborne, with Harry Noakes went down below for the last time.

Also to the rescue went the steamboats, knowing every ripple on the water; Crested Eagle, Royal Eagle, Queen of the Channel, Royal Sovereign, Royal Daffodil and Medway Queen which made seven trips there and back. Disaster struck three of those familiar names, in the shape of the Queen of the Channel, Royal Sovereign and Crested Eagle. Others like the Royal Eagle were more fortunate. She survived altogether forty three dive bombing attacks, having become an anti-aircraft vessel and making three trips to Dunkirk, bringing home some 3,000 servicemen.

Soon afterwards, Southend became something of a garrison town as parents followed their children into safer areas, for vast armies were just across the water and uniforms were predominant in the town; service men and women, police, firemen and A.R.P. making up the population. On the pier there was a naval sick bay, post office, transport office, pill boxes, with members of the Observer Corps, Maritime regiment, signal station, firemen and of course the pier staff, although the piermaster, Captain Johnson, who at all times ran his charge like a ship, was called up early in 1940, for work with the Marine Salvage Department and not released until January 1st, 1945, when the Ministry of Supply wrote expressing their appreciation of his valuable services. Last to be mentioned but by no means least, were the Trinity House pilots and P.L.A. members who organised the intricate convoy system. Not to be forgotten was that water pipe line from shore to ship carrying over 50,000 tons of the precious liquid along the pier, near the end of which was the balloon deck, where the 'kites' were often prepared before being fitted on ships as an anti-aircraft device. In 1941, the year before they were fitted, there was one great disaster on the river, when the Arnia was mined off Shoeburyness with the loss of 67 lives.

Words were written later which applied then: "Let no one disparage Southend pier, nowhere else in the district is so much history implicit in a single scene." [5] It occupied — and still occupies — this unique position at "the gateway of the Thames". While other piers on the south and east coast were demolished or partly so, like those at Bournemouth, Deal, Folkestone, Redcar, and Ventnor, because of their possible use as enemy landing sites, others did not re-open after the war, as at Folkestone, Plymouth and St. Leonards.

Gradually the tide of war changed and strange things were reported in the river. "Soon from Teddington to Southend pier one began to smell the spirit of attack", as Alan Herbert put it. Down the river in his launch he saw the first completed Phoenix, sixty feet high at Tilbury, which made up the Mulberry harbours. He saw gunboats and tank landing craft and an American tug towing a great drum — "the secret of Pluto, the most fantastic invention of them all; taking the oil across the Channel." No wonder that he wrote "the odour of D-Day hung over every reach".

On the eve of D-Day there were over 200 vessels laying off Southend but in a day or so they had all disappeared to the Normandy beaches. Convoys still sailed with vital war supplies in that last year of war with anticipation of victory in the air, in spite of rockets and "doodle bugs", the desperate action of a man once besotted with success and now overwhelmed by defeat, as the allies got closer and closer to Berlin.

Meanwhile in Parliament, A.P. Herbert, the Member for Oxford University, reminded the house of the gallant service rendered by the men with whom he had served on and about the river. During a debate on war medals he asked that their courage should be recognised in the battle of the Thames, especially those who had served on minesweepers and patrol duties, from Southend to Teddington. He did not succeed in his motion, but the M.P. serving as petty officer had felt strongly about rewarding the men who were his comrades.

In March 1945, residents were allowed to return to the homes that they had evacuated in 1940, taking over in many cases property that had been used to quarter service-men and women. This particularly applied at "H.M.S. West-cliff" where a large area had been requisitioned to accommodate 6,000 naval personnel in 1942. During the rest of World War Two over 50,000 were trained in the Westcliff area.

With the triumph of D-Day there could be no relaxing on the river where traffic was even heavier than before it. More than 130 ships a day passed the pier with a resultant increase in the number of messages; there were 350 signals dealt with every 24 hours by ten operators working in watches.

When the Japanese capitulated on September 2nd, 1945, ending the war, following the example of Germany in the previous May, the pier was demobilised from naval service, returning to its more peaceful pursuits. It was only then, with the return home of local people from the armed services and evacuees, that the majority realised exactly what had been happening on the pier, especially those who read "The War Story of Southend Pier" by A.P. Herbert, and this even applied to those whose work kept them in the district for the whole period of the war. In this booklet there is a foreward by the First Lord of the Admiralty, in which he records his appreciation: . . . . . "Instead of pleasure steamers landing happy families, there came alongside the pier vessels carrying men who were fighting the grimmest sea battle ever." He ends saying "Southend, its pier and Old Father Thames are now resuming their peacetime avocations with increased prestige earned by a job well done. May they long remain undisturbed in playing their part in the recon-struction and recreation of our country." [6]

Over the years there have been many other tributes by those who have recorded the events on the river, none more faithfully than the Port of London Authority: "Sitting in the very porch of London's port, its site of such strategic value has enabled Southend to play no mean part in the long and glorious drama of the Thames. It has harboured the primitive fishing craft of the Trinobantes, the longboats of Alfred and Canute, the galleons of the first Elizabeth, and the little ships for Dunkirk; great vessels of most of the maritime nations, bound to and from the ends of the earth who pass through its channel or anchor off its flats". [7]

FOOTNOTES

1. In 1937 the Royal Air Force Volunteer Reserve was formed, and on October 16th, 1939, enemy aircraft were first destroyed by airmen operating from Rochford. Among the many famous airmen who served here in the defence of Britain were 'Al' Deere and the South African 'Sailor' Malan.

2. Two naval experts came down at once to examine this magnetic mine, because nothing was known of this new fangled device which had caused havoc in the shipping lanes. Winston Churchill was concerned over the lack of knowledge of this particular mine. It was dissected, and after lengthy examination by the bomb disposal squad, counter measures were taken so that it never afterwards had the same effect.

3. 'The War Story of Southend Pier' by A.P. Herbert, p.9. He was famous as a writer and politician, having previously been called to the Bar but he never practised. Alan Patrick Herbert was born in 1890, and wrote for 'Punch' in 1924. He was the author of novels 'The Water Gipsies', 'Holy Deadlock' and others which became popular. He served in Parliament for fifteen years from 1935 as Independent Member for Oxford. Knighted in 1945, he became a Companion of Honour in 1970, the year before he died.

4. The Sunday Times, May 9th, 1965.

5. Thames Estuary by William Addison ch.7, p.125/6

6. The First Lord was A.V. Alexander, late Earl Alexander of Hillsborough (1885-1965)

7. The P.L.A. Monthly. September 1952 no.323, p.180.

Before disaster struck. Showing the pavilion used for ten-pin bowling since 1962, with the 'Golden Hind' in the right foreground. (This new pavilion replaced one that was destroyed by fire in 1959).

Chapter Thirteen

Southend was fortunate in having such a celebrity as Alan Herbert to pay tribute to the river, the pier and its birthplace. It was only to be expected that anything written by this popular author would be successful, and so it proved, with this local story. Selling in thousands, it brought home to the reader exactly what had happened on the Thames during the war, and the publicity was more than welcome to the resort as people were having to re-adjust their lives in a Europe that was still conscious of its need for rationing of vital commodities. This included paper, so that it had to be agreed with the printers of this booklet that a smaller quantity would have to be run off, if the whole order was not obtainable.

Another eminent author who had been born and bred in these parts and grew up with a great love of the place and its institutions was Warwick Deeping, who being the son of a doctor, studied medicine at Cambridge University, then gave it up to write, achieving success with his novel in 1925, which was "Sorrell and Son", relating in it some of his own experiences of World War One. Four of his subsequent books dealt with the locality; the first was "The Dark House", (1941). Southend is the thinly disguised "Southfleet" where he grew up and was able to give his impression of the strict Victorian code of conduct, for "they believed in discipline and enforced it".[1]

He mentions the names of the never-to-be-forgotten Dickens and Thackeray, both of whom had died before he was born in 1877, perhaps because both had relatives living in the district, and his father, Dr Deeping had the invalid wife of the latter under his care for she lived at Leigh.

Warwick Deeping was born at Prospect House, after which he named "The Dark House", which was at the end of the High Street, and afterwards his family moved to nearby Royal Terrace, which he called "Queen's Terrace" and said that it was "Southfleet's Park Lane." No wonder that in all these four books he recalls the pier so often, for he had a perfect view of it from both his early homes. "The old wooden pier", he wrote, straddling half a mile of mud when the tide was out, blinked black and white against the water." It was a very busy scene further down by the loading pier, "at the old town jetty, black brigs and schooners unloaded coal, timber, lime and coke, and took off bricks, potatoes and grain."[2] Then again: "Southfleet pier was a favourite parade ground for those active souls who asked for exercise and the sea wind. It ran for a mile, a straight ribbon of timber carried on great black piles, and bulwarked with wooden railings painted white ... In summer an old horse tram rumbled up and down, passing through a tented structure where a local band made metallic music thrice a week. You could walk here as on the deck of a great ship, with the waves rolling round and under you, and the gulls sailing and screaming, secure from all qualms."[3]

His name for the parish church of St. John's, which he attended with his parents was St. Jude's, and here he found one of the characters he admired most of all in the form of the Rev Thomas Varney. In his recollections of his life here, he wrote of Mr Varney: "There must be many people who remember that little, dark-headed, bright-eyed saint . . . . He lived the life of the Christ he served . . . . He had the inner consciousness, divine conviction, and his humility and modesty were utterly disarming. There are many stories of him, one in which he gave his boots away to a tramp."[4] There was a cot named after this gentleman in the Victoria hospital, in commemoration of his devoted and self sacrificing labours in the hospital, town and neighbourhood.

Mr Varney lived again as the "Mr Gurney" of his novels written in 1942/4, entitled "Slade" and then "Mr Gurney and Mr Slade." In this last named book he describes Marine Parade and the pier through the eyes of Mr Gurney. "Here were old fashioned lodging houses and tea gardens, roistering pubs, watermen in blue jerseys, a black jetty which suggested that Southfleet's famous pier had dropped a pup". (The same thing had been said about the Regency pavilion at Brighton with its domes and pagodas by Sydney Smith — that St. Paul's had dropped a pup)![5]

All this was good for Southend and may have encouraged the new scheme embodied in the Miles report, named after the mayor who devised it, in which it was stated that "the chief commodities the town had to offer were the conditions of physical health and the means of recreation". This plan, like others before it, proposed the development of Victoria Avenue as the new home for the town hall and all local government services. The previous scheme had been shelved in 1938, because of the advent of war, when unemployment in the district was in need of some such large building programme; there being a record number of over 5,000 who had no work. Included in the new plan was the improvement of the foreshore between Leigh and its marshes, reconstruction of the pier hill entrance and a yacht harbour.

The greatest idea of all, still bandied about, came from the piermaster, Captain Johnson, in May, 1950, in which he submitted a plan to enclose the whole of the foreshore from Shoebury to Canvey with the provision of lock gates near the pierhead with a new sea wall. There was also an entertainments complex with hotels and concert halls. The mind boggles at the cost of such a scheme today. It seems all the more unfortunate that this was another plan that was shelved, for it could have revitalised the whole seafront.

The time had been ripe then for such an ambitious project, for the previous year had been a record one for the pier undertaking. Over three million admissions, including steamboat passengers, but out of the blue in March had come the first rumblings of financial difficulties in the council chamber caused by the heavy cost of administration of various departments. The piermaster and the treasurer were asked to investigate and later a special committee met for the same purpose. Powers were given to effect any economics that could be made and put the undertaking on a sound financial basis.

In January, 1952, economics were once more on the agenda, and the possibility of reducing still further the amount provided in salaries and wages meant only one thing. It was decided then to restrict the patrolling activities of the launch 'St. George', so that instead of moving around off the seashore it was to be moored off the pierhead and the crew put on other work.[6] Also to reduce expenditure it was resolved not to repair various buildings on the pier.

In a sudden spell of disaster in February, 1953, all the efforts of the authorities were literally washed away, the result of exceptionally high tides and gale force winds which damaged seafront premises to the extent of an estimated £15,000 for complete restoration. Luckily, valuable plant had been rescued from the Westcliff swimming pool by pier staff, otherwise the bill would have been larger. Low-lying Canvey Island suffered loss of life as well as considerable damage when the island was submerged, yet it seems the Ministry of Health were aware of the possible flooding in setting up a commission on Thames Flood Prevention in June, 1931, to consider the position then. It seems little was done, although Canvey has always been vulnerable, even before a domiciled Dutchman was given one-third of the island in 1622, in return for embanking it.

There was some relief from the gloom fostered by the floods, when, in the summer, came the coronation celebrations for Queen Elizabeth II. The river ceremonials were organised by the P.L.A. and ships from many nations paid their tribute, while as on other special occasions battleships lay off the pier; the 'Vanguard' and aircraft carrier 'Thesus' being the target for boatloads of holiday makers. In the following year special arrangements were made locally to welcome home Her Majesty on her return to England. The B.B.C. took a hand in the royal homecoming and Eric

The disastrous fire at the pierhead on July 29th, 1976 at its height.

Winstone and his band came to the pier to broadcast on May 15th. After the affair the elder brethren of Trinity House wrote of their appreciation of the efficient organisation of the arrangements to welcome the Queen. This letter was sent to the piermaster.

It must have been one of the last letters received by him in his official capacity, for Captain J.C. Johnson, who had been awarded the M.B.E. in January, gave notice of his retirement after the return home of the Queen. He had served on the pier since 1931, when he had been selected for the post out of 289 applicants, so that he was somebody very special. Captain Johnson had saved the undertaking a great deal of money in the postwar years, in buying good secondhand material when new stock was either too costly or unobtainable.

It may have been his success in this field that prompted the official view that the new man should be a master mariner, with experience in commerce and control of staff, consequently the position advertised was for a pier manager, which included besides supervision of the staff, liaison with nautical administrations, licensing of first and second class boatmen, moorings, control of the beach and foreshore from Shoebury to Leigh, swimming pools and sundry items, such as the dredger, loading pier — which was still doing good

business — and life-saving. The other duties including the railway and other electrical equipment was under the care of the deputy.

Since the floods, attention and money had to be paid to the sea defences. Another drain on finances was the request of the operators of the Southend to Sheerness passenger service, who asked for time to pay their licence fee, pointing out that their business had suffered over the ban imposed on dogs being allowed on the pier. Unfortunately they had to sell their boat. Another ban which had a serious effect on the pier's income was the refusal of the Treasury to grant "no passport" facilities to steamboat passengers on continental trips. Imposed in 1953, it had been of great concern to those connected with the pier, for local protests seem to fall on stony ground, while another steamship company notified its inability to continue operating their service because of the restriction. After the Chancellor of the Exchequer had made it plain that there was no point in carrying on discussions with Southend in this matter, the town clerk having strenuously opposed the ban from the beginning, an emergency conference was arranged at Brighton in December, 1954, attended by the town clerk, that old stalwart Alderman White and the pier manager. It was agreed to send a deputation to the Secretary of State for Home Affairs,

A view from the air showing the devastation caused by the fire.

enlist the support of M.P.s and set up a sub-committee to fight for the resumption of "no passport" facilities. All this effort eventually had its reward, when restrictions were lifted in time for the 1956 season. During this period a great deal of money had been lost, although boats like the 'Royal Daffodil' still maintained the link between Southend and the continent.

In spite of the fact there were over one-and-a-half million visitors annually to the pier for the next ten years from 1953, there was still a need to economise. Expenditure accounted for items like the painting of the structure, which in 1953 was said to be several years in arrears. This work was necess-ary as it involved the sub-structure which was below main deck level and it was decided to protect this section by painting on a three-year basis. Another factor was the seeming indifference to war damage claims and the dilatory fashion in which they were settled. It was not until October 20, 1955, that it was reported that repairs to the western annex of the pavilion, damaged early in the war, had been completed and paid for by the War Damages Commission.

About this time several traders had to put up the shutters of their kiosks as they were unable to pay their way. This also applied to the pier arcade where hot seawater baths— which had catered for sportsmen everywhere, especially footballers of famous London clubs — had to suspend operations. With the failure of one such business others went the same wa , It was like some giant snowball which gathered momentum as it went.

It was in this atmosphere that a special meeting took place in August 1958, to discuss the proposed — so many times — yacht harbour on the western side of the pier, covering an area 800 ft by 300 ft. When the estimated cost of £10,000 was raised, all dreams vanished like the hopes of a writer, who suggested a harbour made up of old derelict hulks based on the Hadleigh Ray, and asking £5 for his idea. Then it was the interest aroused in the newly designed catamaran, built mainly at Canvey, which was the latest craft owned by members of yacht clubs who all played their part in the yachting weeks centred at the pierhead, with the annual race to the Nore supervised by the Benfleet Yacht Club. Other clubs in the district beside the venerable Alexandra Y.C. are at Leigh, Thorpe Bay, and Wakering, now joined by the latest recruit in the Halfway Y.C. on Eastern Esplanade. All live in hopes that one day the long cherished yacht marina will come into being.

In the 1966/7 season only 33,466 steamboat passengers came to Southend; a drop of over 50,000, although admissions were still over the million mark. As a result there were no steamers calling at the pier for the next two summers — at least not worth the recording. Then two years later a miserable 4,564 passengers came and went by steamboat, while those using the pier still topped the million, unfortunately for the last time.

The Queen Mother came to Southend in October, 1967, opening the Civic Centre in Victoria Avenue, when all the branches of local government were transplanted under one roof from offices in the Clarence Road and Alexandra Street area. Here police and court buildings are situated, also various departments of the civil service, in multi-story blocks. So that not only the planner's but the poet's dream came true, for the vicar of Southchurch, the Rev. Thomas Archer, had written of this little resort way back in 1794: "Here with prophetic view the bard descries, streets shall extend and lofty domes arise". There are other prophesies and dreams still unfulfilled; like the one by the mayor in 1913, who thought that in the next twenty years the town would be a city with it's own lord mayor. In the same year the independent urban council of Shoeburyness met to consider the provision of a harbour and quay, plus the added attraction of a fish market.

The last few years in the life of the pier have been both difficult and controversial. In the 1970/1 season there were less than one million admissions, so other means had to be found to attract the public. This was provided by a nationally known concern who eventually rented the pierhead facilities and added to them, in the form of a night club and licensed premises. All this was destroyed in the devastating fire of July 29th, 1976, leaving, for the time being, only the memories. Memories of Adam Seebold playing with the orchestra before the war and jovial Ben Oakley doing the same thing after it, in the halcyon days when waxworks and puppet shows, concert parties, yacht races and the never-to-be-forgotten steamboats drew over three million people in one year, to sample the pleasures of the pier, while others fished

Deck level picture showing the twisted metal and rubble.

or listened to the band or watched the shipping. Nearly all brought to the end by the electric railway which has made its last journey until safety repairs to the track have been made.

It is no consolation that other piers have gone the same way. Just as the poverty of the people nearly forced it out of business over one hundred years ago; now our affluence threatens the life of the pier. The car and aeroplane are taking people further afield.

The fortunate geographical position of the town and the strategic value of the pier during World War Two, at the mouth of one of the most important rivers in the world, should not be forgotten for the need of both could arise again. Remember the words of A.P. Herbert in concluding his story of those momentous days: "Tell your children about it in the years to come, as you sit in the sun and listen to the band and watch the ships go by. Make them, if you can, see beyond. Let them look up London river to London, and see this pier as the sentinal at the gate, interested in everything that comes and goes . . . . . Tell them the things this pier has seen — the ships barking back at the bombers out there — the dog fights overhead — the ships hobbling home with holes in their sides — the little boats for Dunkirk streaming out and back — the blazing tankers — the gunboats running for rest — the falling planes — the ships gathered for D—day, with more

View from the water, again showing the distorted metal of the pier structure The lifeboat can be seen dealing with still smouldering timbers.

ships up river as far as the eye could see . . . . . But above all, tell them the convoy work went on. London was fed. The ships came and went. The battle of the Thames was won. And Southend remains for all to enjoy."(7)

Like most Southenders, A.P. Herbert could not visualise the pier ever not being available for all to enjoy, for it is part and parcel of the town. Meeting strangers away from Southend it is invariably the first topic to be discussed, and in the past it has been described with a feeling of pride. Perhaps the pier may have a new role in the future, as the western boundary of a proposed sea/air port or yacht marina, or as the headquarters of a maritime museum, in which much that is nostagically remembered by millions can be displayed. There one could see the old anchor presented to the town after the war; the mayoral chair made out of the old wooden pier in 1892; film made of the installation of new pier trains and

A 'walkway' provided over the damaged decking to allow access to and from the boats.

bought by the corporation in October 1957; the honours board now at the civic centre; pictures of the old steamboats; of Trinity House and P.L.A. vessels which have all played their part in the history of what has been designated " the longest pleasure pier in the world". [8]

If all else fails, would it not be possible for some enterprising concern, such as the National Trust, which has been called the " caretaker of our heritage", to take over the care of this most famous of all piers, as it has with the isolated island of Lundy, and famous landmarks like the white cliffs of Dover and the Thameside meadows of Runnymede? [9]

FOOTNOTES

1. The Dark House by Warwick Deeping. p.35.
2. The Dark House by Warwick Deeping. p.47.
3. The Dark House by Warwick Deeping. p.148.
4. St. John's Church by Warwick Deeping. p.9. In his fourth book on the locality Caroline Terrace (1955) he calls the town by its original name South End and refers to the church as St. Johns.
5. Mr. Gurney and Mr. Slade by Warwick Deeping. p.17.
6. The launch was later sold for £2,000.
7. The War Story of Southend Pier by A.P. Herbert. p.32.
8. The Guinness Book of Records. The pier being 2,360 yards long (2.157.984 metres.
9. The Reader's Digest, January 1976.

APPENDIX

Chronological history of the pier

1829   At a meeting to discuss the bill tenders were invited for 90 English oak trees, one of which was used on the 18th July when the first pile was driven into place, a week before the foundation-stone was laid.

1830   It was announced in May at the first annual gathering of the pier management committee that nearly 600 ft had been completed. When opened to the public the admission charge was two pence a day or two shillings monthly.

1831   In October, Alderman (later Sir) William Heygate held a public breakfast on the pier.

1833   The first fair was held here in aid of the building fund for St John's church.

1834   By this time there was an upper platform for passengers and a lower platform for the landing of goods.

1835   Nearly £20,000 spent on the project and another £6,000 borrowed.

1838   Southend said to be the only resort where water was completely salt.

1845   A railway company, seeing the potential of the resort, was eager to build a track to Southend, and belatedly to construct a pier.

1846   Pier now a mile-and-a-quarter in length, which did not stop it being sold at a loss of £25,000, when it fetched £17,000.

1854   It was confirmed that Trinity House had the exclusive rights of lighting, and placing buoys around the coast.

1855   A year before the railway line was opened, fares by steamboat to London from Southend was six shillings and sixpence, and by coach fifteen shillings. (Railways charged one penny a mile).

1859   The London, Tilbury and Southend Railway Company who had a financial interest in the pier also developed Clifftown, west of Royal Terrace as a housing estate.
       Because gun firing on Plumstead marshes interfered with shipping on the Thames, the Royal Artillery moved to Shoeburyness.

1861   Control of the local yacht races exercised from the pierhead.

1865   Mr George Vandervord, bargeowner and chairman of the local board (1873-8) bought Rayleigh House from Lord Rayleigh.

1866   James Heygate, son of the pier's promoter, became the first chairman of the local board, while a Mr Gregson was appointed clerk at £40 per annum.

1869   The Rev. F. Thackeray bought No 10 Royal Terrace for £2,000 at the sale of the Scratton estates, when the Royal hotel was sold for £4,000.

1873   After some wrangling the local board had to pay £12,000 for the pier. A medical officer was appointed for the town at £5 per annum; "except in a case of an epidemic", when he would be considered to be worth more.

1875   Town provided with a fire escape, with the promise of a fire engine. Two years later the fire brigade was formed. A visitor complained at 'indecent mixed bathing', when he saw two men and a woman in the water. He was told to mind his own business.

1876   There were heated debates over the high and low level entrance to the pier. Voters for the high level won the day and that is its present position.

1877   Yacht race around English coast, with the start and finish at the pier.

1878   Another of the Heygate family – J.U. – becomes chairman of the local board.

1881   There was an attempt to form a company, using the 'Great Britain' steamship moored off the pier, as a floating hotel and sanatorium.

1883   Maritime signalling for Lloyds started July 30. The first county councillor for the Southend division of Essex was Mr (later Sir) Lloyd Wise, chairman of the local board, who obtained a favourable report on the pier.

1885   New tollhouse built and a new pier decided upon. Act for this purpose passed two years later, to replace wooden structure. Sir James Brunlees appointed engineer.

1888   Construction of pier with cast iron piles was started. At the same time electric railway tracks laid down by Messrs Crompton of Chelmsford.

1889   Existing pier opened although not completed, like the railway track; over which an experimental run was made of about three-quarters of a mile.

1890   Now the railway was finished, being 1.25 miles long. Three-coach train in operation. Fire broke out on old pier which contained materials for the new one being built alongside. Salvation Army bought land at Hadleigh, establishing a farm colony there, having already chapels in Shoebury and Southend. William Booth's book "In darkest England and the way out" shows a chart of this colony and the area. Over the picture of the pier are the words: "Whitechapel by Sea".

1891   So popular had the railway become and so many bogus claims made regarding 'accidents' that a plain clothes man was employed to travel on the pier trains.

1892   Southend became a municipal borough and included the pier in its coat of arms.

1893   Thirteen unlicensed boatmen plied for hire on Whit Monday and were prosecuted. Three bathing machine proprietors lucky enough to be licensed were granted renewals; they were Messrs Absalom, Saunders and Ingram. Mr Gilson refused to move a boat from the beach, so the new council did it for him.

1895   Telephone installed between pier and fire station. Competition by the public invited for proposed pier hill buildings, with a first prize of £20. Mr Townsend of the Army and Navy public house, required to pay five shillings for his flagstaff. Meeting place of many London clubs when situated on the Embankment, "The Palace Floating Swimming Baths" came to Southend, where there was a disturbance among the ratepayers at having to borrow large sums to pay for it.

1897   The pier extension was built and opened in the following year. This had been necessary over the problem of 'silting up'. The cost was £20,000. On September 1 at the request of the post office, the signal station began to operate as a public telegraph office. Southchurch enters the borough.

1899   Addition to loop on electric railway. Now twelve cars in use.

1902   With the installation of the council's electricity generating station, the pier plant was sold. The water chute was opened on the east side of pier. News reel of the South African war shown at the Pavilion.

1904   The Metropole Hotel came into being, known as the Palace Hotel and overlooking the pier.

1906   Through the generosity of Andrew Carnegie, American steel millionaire, the Central Library was built.
The Thames Conservancy Board reported progress in deepening the lower river, between Gravesend and the Nore.

1908   On July 25 the upper deck of the pier extension was opened. The fire brigade which had carried out exercises on the pier, won the National Fire Brigade championship.

1912   Princess Louise, daughter of the late Queen Victoria, came to open the new wing of Victoria Hospital.

1913   Leigh entered the borough, which in the following year became a county borough.

1914   Signal station on the pier taken over by the Admiralty.

1915   Permission given for 'little Russian flags' to be sold on the pier. The Southend Amateur Angling Society objected to the practice of certain anglers on the pier using two or more rods or lines, so taking up most of the space and fish.

1918   In terms of damage and war materials lost; the worst disaster of the war occurred on March 28, when ammunition dumps at Shoeburyness exploded. No lives were lost and the place was evacuated, people walking along the beach to Southend and safety.

1919   On May 10 a plane landed newspapers by parachute near the pier.

1920   National Federation of Discharged and Demobilised Sailors and Soldiers called on council to discharge three female employees. Licensed watermen represented by the N.U.G.W. requested that no jetty should be allowed to anyone not a ratepayer or resident of twelve months.

1922   In February, Sir John Brunlees, presented his original drawings of the Pier Pavilion, of which he was the architect, to the council. Permission of Trinity House was obtained to the request of the Essex Fishermen's Union, Leigh branch, that new lights on Leigh cliffs should be increased, and altered to bring them in line with the Low-way buoy. Sanction was also given to a Captain Lawson Smith to give exhibition of 'submarine diving' in connection with a film being made. Royal standard used in connection with the visit of George V in yachting week, given to the council.

1924   In February, the P.L.A. requested that a tidal ball be fixed on pier which would enable pilots of deep-laden ships to proceed with confidence. One of many such visits made by the mayor of Islington, when he brought one hundred orphaned children of ex-servicemen to Southend, and was given free facilities for them on the pier.

1926	General Strike paralysed the country. Southend and district relieved with the opening of Ford's at Dagenham.
1927	New additions made to the upper deck of the extension. Piermaster reported that a number of London football clubs were using the hot seawater baths.
1928	Piermaster authorised to post notices on details of guns firing from Shoebury and the Isle of Grain, which had already sewn the seeds of partial deafness in a few local ears. Mayor's unemployment committee reported 1,299 workless in the borough. Work for thirty promised on pier.
1929	Double railway track running length of pier. Automatic signals installed. Prince George Extension opened at a cost of £57,700. Before the year was out an upper deck was approved.
1930	Because of severe flooding in London, the L.C.C. was given authority to erect a tide gauge at the shore end of the pier, connecting up with the Central Police Station. The present extension was completed. Now 2,360 yards or 1 mile, 2 furlongs, 160 yards. The longest pleasure pier in the world. The mayor of Southend proposed an ambitious plan for the foreshore at a cost of over £4 million. Owing to unsettled state of the country there was no hope of carrying it out.
1931	Mr Louis Tussaud, of Harrow, made an application to use corner of the upper deck for his waxworks. Assent given for five years.
1933	The Southend Antiquarian and Historical Society reported that the smaller and older of the historic Crowstones bore an inscription that it was now impossible to read. The P.L.A. stated that it could not be restored or repaired because of its condition. It now stands in Priory Park, the gift of the P.L.A. Radio Normandie broadcast on Whit Sunday items by the pier orchestra and Pavilion dance band. In June, 100 French schoolboys were allowed free on the pier. German schoolboys had also been allowed the same privilege two years previously, while staying in the town. To add to the variety of visitors, before that members of the South African Farmers' Association had been on the pier. Shoebury and Eastwood enter the borough, making up the family.
1934	The P.L.A. gave notice of their intention to allow the erection of 'certain piers and landing places'. A letter circularised from the pier company, suggesting the formation of a Pier Owners' Association was received, but no action was taken.
1935	Council bought Leigh cliffs from Salvation Army for £33,500. Illuminations begin. Airport opened by Secretary of State.
1938	Council approved scheme for new Civic Centre, law courts, police and fire headquarters, all costing under £2000,000 with government help.
1939	World War Two begins on September 3 and until September 9 the public were allowed to use the pier. The navy took over August 25.
1945	Before the end of the war, the mayor of Southend was asked formally to re-open the pier on March 27. Naval Control present ancient anchor to the town. Westcliff and Nore yacht clubs amalgamate under Thames Estuary Y.C. The P.L.A. require all lights exhibited before September 1939 to be re-installed.
1947	In May, the B.B.C. broadcast "Down Your Way" from 'Royal Eagle', with commentary on arrival at the pier by Wynford Vaughan Thomas.
1948	Twelve turnstiles used on the pier bought by Southend United F.C. Prompt action by Mr W. Ward on duty at the pierhead, saved the life of a member of the crew of the barge 'Thelma' during a gale. Mr Ward was awarded the Pier life saving medal.
1949	The courtesy of the pier staff made an immediate impact on a Mr Wallace, which influenced him to become a resident. Pier and fore-shore illuminations restored to pre-war power. The lord mayor of London and Southend's mayor drove the first of the new electric trains. This was the most successful of all seasons — over three million admissions including steamboat passengers.
1950	This season over two-and-a-half million people used the pier. Local firm provided three pianos at £1 per week.
1951	Another good summer, the total admissions being 2,325,148. Revival of whitebait festival.
1952	Just over two million admissions.
1953	A total of 1,848,027 used the pier. Rising prices put up luncheon costs on pier from 3s 6d to 3s 9d.
1954	Flitch trial held on the pier, for local married couples.

1956	Shipping exhibition on the pier attracted nearly 100,000.
1957	Film made of pier buildings and trains sold to the corporation.
1958	As the result of market research carried out, great majority were well satisfied with pier and wide range of entertainment.
1959	The berthing master lived on pier until his retirement in December. Pavilion built in 1889, gutted by ninety-minute blaze.
1962	Ten-pin bowling alley opened on the site of the Pavilion.
1965	In May, the mayor unveiled a plaque to commemorate the seventy-fifth aniversary of pier railway.
1967	There were no steamboat companies operating from the pier to coastal resorts this summer, which coincided with the opening of the Civic Centre in Victoria Avenue by the Queen Mother.
1969	Steamboats this year brought 4,564 to the pier, the total admissions being 1,020,807. There are no more recorded boat passengers.
1973	The last figure for the public using the pier is 696,159, there having been a deterioration under the million mark since 1970.
1976	The fire on the pierhead in July put the pier out of business.
1979	Trains have stopped running, the track being declared unsafe and Mr. Derek Tyler, the chief foreshore inspector and once in charge of the pier management, has resigned.

ACKNOWLEDGMENTS

The author wishes to thank the following people and organisations for their help in supplying pictures and information:

The Honourable Charles Strutt for loaning me his family history. Mr. Don Ronan for his information on his grandfather, the late William Bradley, the old pierhead keeper. The Central Reference Library staff for their ever willing searches; also the Southend and Chelmsford Record Offices. The Trinity House Lighthouse Service. House of Lords Record Office. The Guildhall Library. The editor of the Southend Standard. Fred Robinson for information on the Southend lifeboat and pier. Mike Shorter for reproducing many of the illustrations. Derek Tyler, former pier manager and chief foreshore inspector. The Southend branch of the Essex Record Office and the Southend Libraries and Museum Committees. The Royal National Lifeboat Institution. P.L.A. Southend Pictorial Air Services. Daily Mail. London Transport (Underground), and Southend-on-Sea Borough Council.

BIBLIOGRAPHY

Adamson, Simon, H.	Seaside Piers (1977).
Addison, William	Thames Estuary (1954).
Armstrong, W.	The Thames from its Rise to the Nore (1887).
Barrett, C.R.B.	The Trinity House of Deptford Stroud (1893).
Benton, Philip	History of the Rochford Hundred (1886).
Bryant, Arthur	Samuel Pepys, Saviour of the Navy (1953).
Burtt, Frank	Steamers of the Thames and Medway.
Burrows, J.W.	Southend-on-Sea and District (1909).
Burrows, V.E.	The Tramways of Southend (1965).
Cassell and Co.	The Thames and its Story.
Deeping, Warwick	St John's Parish Church (1950).
Deeping, Warwick	The Dark House (1941).
Deeping, Warwick	Mr Gurney and Mr Slade (1944).
Deeping Warwick	Slade (1943).
Deeping Warwick	Caroline Terrace (1955)
Dickens, Charles	Dictionary of the Thames (1880)
Dobree and Manwaring	The Floating Republic.
Glennie, Donald	Our Town (1947).
Granville, A.B.	The Spas of England (reprinted 1971).
Herbert, Alan	War Story of Southend Pier (1945).
Herbert, John	The Port of London (1947).
Malster, Robert	Wreck and Rescue on the Essex Coast (1968).
Mead, Hilary P.	Trinity House.
P.L.A. Monthly.	
Pollitt, William	The Rise of Southend (1957).
Southend	Proceedings of Council and Committees (1893).
Southend	Antiquarian and Historical Society Transactions.
Southend	Standard (1873).
Strutt, Hon. Charles	The Strutt Family of Terling.
Strutt, William Goodday	The Strutt Papers (1829-38).
	(Now in the Southend branch of the E.R.O.).
Tawke, Miss	Recollections of Southend (1912).
Turner, E.S.	Taking the Cure (1967).

INDEX

(Folios in bold type indicate illustrations)